Essential Series

Springer

London
Berlin
Heidelberg
New York
Barcelona
Hong Kong
Milan
Paris
Singapore
Tokyo

Ian Chivers

Essential Linux *fast*

 Springer

Ian Chivers BSc, PGCEd, MSc
The Computer Centre, Kings College, Strand, London WC2R 2LS

Series Editor
John Cowell, BSc (Hons), MPhil, PhD
Department of Computer Science, De Montfort University, The Gateway,
Leicester LE1 9BH

British Library Cataloguing in Publication Data
Chivers, I.D. (Ian David), 1952-
  Essential Linux fast. – (Essentials)
  1. Linux (Computer file)
  I. Title II. Linux fast
  005.4.'469
ISBN 1852334088

Library of Congress Cataloging-in-Publication Data
Chivers, I.D. (Ian David), 1952-
  Essential Linux fast/Ian Chivers.
    p. cm.
  Includes bibliographical references.
  ISBN 1-85233-408-8
  1. Linux. 2. Operating systems (Computers) I. Title.
QA76.76.O63 C4585 2001
005.4'32--dc21   2001020555

ISBN 1-85233-408-8 Springer-Verlag London Berlin Heidelberg
A member of BertelsmannSpringer Science+Business Media GmbH
http://www.springer.co.uk

Typeset by Mac Style, Scarborough, N. Yorkshire
Printed and bound at The Cromwell Press, Trowbridge, Wiltshire
34/3830-543210 Printed on acid-free paper SPIN 1078669

Contents

Chapter 1

Overview

'Don't panic'

Douglas Adams, *The Hitch-Hiker's Guide to the Galaxy*

 The aim of this chapter is to provide a background to the rest of the material in the book.

Assumptions

It is assumed that you have your own PC with a version of Windows installed, have a basic familiarity with DOS, Windows and the hardware, and are not scared by the idea of taking the case off and having a look inside. It is also assumed that you are interested in installing Linux either on a system on its own or have it coexist with Windows, so that you get the best of both worlds.

What is Linux?

The common perception most people have of Linux is a free Unix-type operating system. In fact it is made up of two major strands that were independent. The first component historically to be developed was by the GNU project and its efforts to develop a free Unix operating system. This work was driven by Richard Stallman. The second component was the development of the kernel for an operating system. This was driven by Linus Torvalds.

The GNU Project

The GNU project's aim was to develop a free Unix operating system. They started in 1983 and by the early 1990s had put together the whole system apart from a working kernel.

The kernel

At the same time a kernel was being developed as a hobby by Linus Torvalds who was a student at the University of Helsinki. He started in 1991 and by the time that the GNU project was nearing completion he had it developed.

GNU Linux

Combining the Linux kernel with the almost complete GNU system resulted in a complete operating system, a Linux-based GNU system.

So what most people call Linux is in fact better called GNU Linux. One major distributor found that 3% of the source code was the kernel and about 28% GNU source code.

This system has been under development ever since. The January 25th version 1999 was 2.2. Linux is an independent POSIX implementation and includes:

- multitasking
- virtual memory
- shared libraries
- demand loading
- memory management
- TCP/IP networking.

It started out running on the Intel 80386 processor but now runs on quite a wide range of hardware, including

- Intel
- Amd
- Cyrix
- Digital Alpha,
- Sparc
- UltraSparc
- PPC
- StrongARM

and more are in the pipeline.

What is POSIX?

POSIX stands for Portable Operating System Interface, and is an IEEE standard designed to facilitate application portability. POSIX is an attempt by a consortium of vendors to create a single standard version of UNIX.

What is Unix?

Unix itself was originally a trademark for a family of computer operating systems developed at Bell Laboratories, and, later, Unix System Laboratories, Inc.

The story begins with Ken Thompson and a PDP-7 minicomputer in 1969. He and his colleagues wanted to develop a working environment suitable for programming research. The second version ran on the unprotected PDP-11/20, and the third added multiprogramming and ran on a range of PDP-11 computers.

They were influenced by the work that had been done in the development of the Multics system. This was a collaboration between Bell Labs, General Electric (Honeywell) and the Massachusetts Institute of Technology.

The original kernel was about 10,000 lines of C and 1,000 lines of assembler. It eventually made its way out of Bell Labs and started to take off.

In 1980 the US DoD funded Berkeley University to develop Unix systems from a small timesharing system to one suitable for a distributed computing environment. BSD 4.1 supported a large address space, demand-paged virtual memory, a fast and powerful file system, inter-process communication, network support and a new shell.

Unix has now established itself as one of the most widely used operating systems in the world, and it runs on a very wide range of computer hardware.

Brief history of networking: TCP/IP and the Internet

TCP/IP forms the basis for networking. TCP/IP refers to a suite of communications protocols. The main two are:

- Transmission Control Protocol (TCP)

and

- Internet Protocol (IP).

The origin of the development of these protocols starts in 1969 with the funding by the Advanced Research Projects Agency (ARPA) of the development of an experimental packet switching network (ARPANET).

This became operational in 1975 and the responsibility for administering it passed to the Defence Communications Agency (DCA).

1983 saw the adoption of the TCP/IP protocols as Military Standards (MIL STD) and the funding of the implementation of them in BSD Unix. It was at this time that the term Internet came into existence.

1985 saw the National Science Foundation (NSF) create NSFNet and links to the Internet, and scientists and engineers start to take advantage of what it had to offer.

We will come back to cover some of the simple technical aspects of TCP/IP that are required to network a Linux system in a later chapter.

The rest of the book

The first part of the book looks at some of the preparatory work you need to do before installing Linux. There is also coverage of some of the options that are open to you.

There is then coverage of a number of installations so that you can see for yourself some of the ways that you can install Linux.

There is then brief coverage of the core elements of using a Linux system.

Bibliography

Linux

http://www.linux.org/

The place to start. The linux.org domain was registered in May 1994 by Michael McLagan. It was intended to act as a central clearing house for information and the promotion of Linux. It operates as a not-for-profit business and is located in Laurel, Maryland USA.

GNU

http://gnu.org

The place to start. Follow the links to the sections by Richard Stallman. He has a lot to answer for!

Unix

Bell System, The Bell System Technical Journal, July/August 1978, Volume 57, No. 6, Part 2.

- This provides a historical look at the development of Unix, upon which Linux is based. Contents include:
  - Ritchie, D.M. & Thompson, K., The Unix Time-Sharing System.

- ○ Thompson, K., Unix Implementation
- ○ Ritchie, D.M., A Retrospective.
- ○ Bourne, S.R., The Unix Shell.
- ○ Ritchie, D.M., Johnson, S.C., Lesk, M.E. & Kernighan, B.W., The C Programming Language.

Operating systems

Deitel, H.M., *Operating Systems*, Addison Wesley.

- Good general coverage of operating systems principles, with case studies. The second edition I have is slightly dated.

TCP/IP

Hunt, C., *TCP/IP Network Administration*, O'Reilly

- Good introduction to TCP/IP. Typical O'Reilly book!

Acknowledgements

I've had help from a number of people whilst installing Linux and writing this book.

I'd first like to thank Andy Thomas at Imperial College for helping out with some strange problems with a 3Com card and boot prom.

I'm also grateful to John Packer at King's on the networking and security side. Given a choice of cables I managed to pick the one duff one. Being able to see the machine from other systems but not access the network at all from this system confused me to say the least. John is responsible for the network at King's and warned me about the security problems systems on the network.

Chats with Neal Faulks and Andy Harper also helped keep me sane when things went wrong. Knowing that other people are having similar problems is reassuring.

Chapter

2

Linux Versions

The aim of this chapter is to look briefly at the various versions of Linux that are available.

There are a large number of Linux versions available. The best place to start looking is:

- http://www.linux.org/

There are three major flavours that can be used, to install from:

- using an ftp server
- free/cheap CD-Rom
- CD-Rom/book bundle.

Given the size of Linux we will only consider the second and third options. We will look at Red Hat Linux and SuSe Linux. Both are available as a free or cheap CD-Rom version and as a book/CD bundle with technical support.

Starting with the above URL follow the links to a local supplier. In the UK I've used:

- http://www.linuxemporium.co.uk/

Similar distributors can be found worldwide.

Red Hat

The following is the main Red Hat site.

- http://www.redhat.com/

For the latest information visit their site. Red Hat distributions change over time. We will look at a number of distributions.

Red Hat 7

Release 7 comes in the following versions:

- Standard
- Deluxe
- Professional server.

Each of the above comes as a boxed set with manuals and technical support. The standard edition comes with an Installation Guide; the deluxe version comes with an Installation Guide and Getting Started Guide.

Red Hat also provide CD images available for download as well as all the individual files in the release. These are:

- Red Hat Linux 7.0 installation CDs for x86 (2 CDs)
- Red Hat Linux 7.0 source CD (1 CD)
- Red Hat Linux 7.0 documentation CD (1 CD)
- Red Hat Linux 7.0 powertools x86 CD (1 CD)

In the UK these are available from the Linux Emporium for around £10.00.

Red Hat 6.2

Release 6.2 came in the following versions:

- Standard
- Professional.

Each of these came as a boxed set with manuals and technical support.

Release 6.2 also came as a cheap CD set. This offered the following installation options:

- Workstation
- Server
- Custom
- Upgrade.

These were available from Linux Emporium at very low cost.

SuSe

The following are some useful web addresses for SuSe:

- http://www.suse.com

- http://www.suse.co.uk/
- http://www.suse.de

Up to date information about their products can be found there. As with Red Hat the SuSe distributions change over time. We will look at a couple of distributions.

SuSe 7

This exists in three main versions:

- Personal
- Professional
- Subscription or Update.

The scope of the Update software is the same as for SuSE Linux 7.0 Professional, but instead of the detailed SuSE manual, it provides information on the most important enhancements.

A single CD version is also available. If you have a system that can boot from CD then this is a cheap and simple option. We will come back to this option later in this chapter.

The Personal version comes with an Installation Guide, Applications Guide and Configuration Guide. The Professional version comes with a Reference Guide.

SuSe 6.4

This distribution was available in a number of versions. They were similar to the Red Hat offerings.

Overview of the installation options

The installation options fall into the following broad categories:

- dual boot
  - boot and run from CD on a DOS/Windows PC
  - a partitionless install
  - dedicate a partition to Linux on a disk with DOS and Windows installed
  - dedicate a whole disk to Linux in a system with DOS and Windows installed
- single boot
  - boot from hard disk.

The installation you choose will depend on the system you have and how much time and effort you want to put in. On older and slower systems with relatively small amounts of memory, e.g. P75, 32Mb memory, 2Gb hard disk, I would go for a single operating system installation with Linux booting from the hard disk.

On faster and more powerful systems the other options become available. On a PII 350 with 192Mb of memory and 48-speed CD you can run Linux quite well off the CD.

If you don't want to bother with learning about partitioning you may choose a partitionless install.

If you have a spare disk then dedicating the whole drive to Linux is an option.

If your hard drive is big enough then you have the option of dedicating one of the partitions to Linux.

Chapter 4 will actually provide details of installing using all of the above ways on a range of systems.

Bibliography

http://www.linux.org/

- The place to start.

http://www.linuxemporium.co.uk/

- Very good UK distributor.

http://www.redhat.com/

- Red Hat's home address.

http://www.suse.de/en/

- SuSe English home page.

http://www.suse.com/

- US home page.

Chapter 3

The Preliminaries

The aim of this chapter is to look briefly at some of the preparatory work you need to do before installing Linux.

It is assumed that you have already got a PC with a version of Windows installed. This makes it easier to determine reasonably accurate details about the hardware.

How to find out hardware details about your system

This will depend on what version of Windows you have.

Windows 95, 98, NT

Choose Start → Settings → Control Panel. The following screen shot shows this.

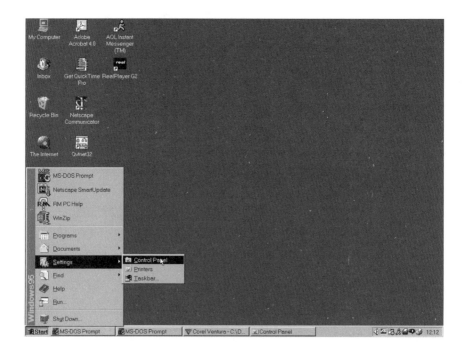

This will bring up the following Window:

Then choose System. This will bring up the following:

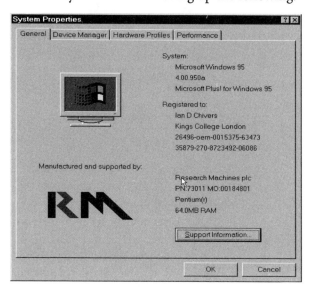

Clicking on the Device Manager tab will bring up the following:

Choose Print and this should bring up the following:

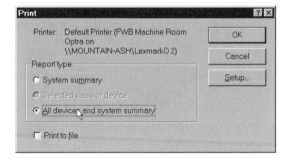

Choose All devices and System summary and print. This will generate a several-page report about the installed devices on your system. Keep it for reference.

Windows 3.x

If you have an earlier version of Windows I would recommend running the MSD.EXE utility. This will produce a several-page report on the system. Again keep this for reference. It is then possible to go to the manufacturer's website and download the appropriate drivers.

Hardware and associated manuals

The first thing to do is check your hardware against the Linux-supported hardware. You should have details of the following as a minimum:

- Keyboard
- Mouse
- Hard drive(s)
- CD-Rom drive
- Monitor
- Graphics card
- Network card.

Have a look to see what manuals and documentation came with the system. Hopefully you will have the manuals for the devices you have installed. Look also for the configuration and diagnostic disks for each device. It may be necessary to visit the manufacturer's website to get the latest drivers, and configuration and diagnostic programs.

I recommend going to the Red Hat and SuSe sites to find details of the latest supported hardware.

I found the SuSe site easier to navigate.

Your DOS and Windows distribution disks

The age of your system and what version of DOS you have will determine what you need to do to create a set of recovery disks. You will need these in the event of a problem with the Linux install that causes you to need to reinstall Windows.

With earlier versions of Windows it should include

- a set of DOS floppies
- a Windows CD
- one or more CDs with specialist device drivers
- one or more application CDs, e.g. Microsoft Word.

With more recent machines and versions of Windows you may be able to boot from the CD and simply reinstall from that.

Making boot floppies

If you don't have a boot floppy then type

- format a: /s

at the DOS prompt. This will format the disk and install all the files needed to enable you to boot from this floppy.

Try

- dir a:

to see what has been included.

Then try

- dir /a:

to see what hidden files are installed.

What additional files are needed?

You will need to add some additional files to this disk. The following is a directory listing of the windows\command directory from a Windows 95 machine.

```
ANSI      SYS      9,719    24/08/96   11:11   ANSI.SYS
ATTRIB    EXE     15,252    24/08/96   11:11   ATTRIB.EXE
CHKDSK    EXE     28,096    24/08/96   11:11   CHKDSK.EXE
CHOICE    COM      5,175    24/08/96   11:11   CHOICE.COM
COUNTRY   SYS     27,094    24/08/96   11:11   COUNTRY.SYS
```

```
DEBUG      EXE      20,554   24/08/96   11:11   DEBUG.EXE
DELTREE    EXE      19,019   24/08/96   11:11   DELTREE.EXE
DISKCOPY   COM      21,975   24/08/96   11:11   DISKCOPY.COM
DISPLAY    SYS      17,175   24/08/96   11:11   DISPLAY.SYS
DOSKEY     COM      15,495   24/08/96   11:11   DOSKEY.COM
DRVSPACE   BIN      65,271   24/08/96   11:11   DRVSPACE.BIN
DRVSPACE   SYS       2,135   24/08/96   11:11   DRVSPACE.SYS
EDIT       COM      69,886   24/08/96   11:11   EDIT.COM
EDIT       HLP      10,790   24/08/96   11:11   EDIT.HLP
EGA        CPI      58,870   24/08/96   11:11   EGA.CPI
EXTRACT    EXE      46,656   01/05/97   12:14   EXTRACT.EXE
FC         EXE      20,574   24/08/96   11:11   FC.EXE
FDISK      EXE      63,116   24/08/96   11:11   FDISK.EXE
FIND       EXE       6,658   24/08/96   11:11   FIND.EXE
FORMAT     COM      49,543   01/05/97   12:14   FORMAT.COM
KEYB       COM      19,927   24/08/96   11:11   KEYB.COM
KEYBOARD   SYS      34,566   24/08/96   11:11   KEYBOARD.SYS
KEYBRD2    SYS      31,942   24/08/96   11:11   KEYBRD2.SYS
LABEL      EXE       9,324   24/08/96   11:11   LABEL.EXE
MEM        EXE      32,146   24/08/96   11:11   MEM.EXE
MODE       COM      29,271   24/08/96   11:11   MODE.COM
MORE       COM      10,471   24/08/96   11:11   MORE.COM
MOVE       EXE      27,235   24/08/96   11:11   MOVE.EXE
MSCDEX     EXE      25,473   24/08/96   11:11   MSCDEX.EXE
NLSFUNC    EXE       6,940   24/08/96   11:11   NLSFUNC.EXE
SCANDISK   EXE     142,353   01/05/97   12:14   SCANDISK.EXE
SCANDISK   INI       7,332   24/08/96   11:11   SCANDISK.INI
SORT       EXE      25,882   24/08/96   11:11   SORT.EXE
START      EXE       9,216   24/08/96   11:11   START.EXE
SUBST      EXE      17,904   24/08/96   11:11   SUBST.EXE
SYS        COM      18,967   24/08/96   11:11   SYS.COM
XCOPY      EXE       3,878   24/08/96   11:11   XCOPY.EXE
XCOPY32    EXE      41,472   24/08/96   11:11   XCOPY32.EXE
```

You will need at least

- edit.com
- FDISK.exe
- format.com

Autoexec.bat and config.sys

I would recommend having a look at both the autoexec.bat file and the config.sys files. These are found in the root directory of your C drive. The following are the contents of an autoexec.bat file and config.sys file for one of the systems I work on.

```
SET TZ=GMTGDT
mode con codepage prepare=((850) C:\WINDOWS\COMMAND\ega.cpi)
mode con codepage select=850
keyb uk,,C:\WINDOWS\COMMAND\keyboard.sys
DOSkey
set ROOTDIR=C:/unix
set HOME=C:/unix
set TMPDIR=f:/temp
set tmp=f:\temp
set temp=f:\temp
set SHELL=C:/unix/mksnt/sh.exe
set LOGNAME=mks
Set NWLANGUAGE=ENGLISH
rem SET IMNINSTSRV=d:\IMNNQ_95
SET
PATH=C:\NOVELL\CLIENT32;C:\UNIX\MKSNT;C:\WINDOWS;C:\WINDOWS\
COMMAND;C:\UT;C:\WIN32APP\SALFORD;F:\JDK1.2.2\BIN;.;C:\RBTI\
RBWIN65\RSTRUC
rem SET IMNINSTSRV=d:\IMNNQ_95
```

and

```
device=C:\WINDOWS\COMMAND\display.sys con=(ega,,1)
Country=044,850,C:\WINDOWS\COMMAND\country.sys
shell=c:\command.com /p /e:32000
FILES=100
```

CD-Rom drivers

Make sure that you have the CD-Rom drivers for your PC. Windows does not require these to be installed in your autoexec.bat file or config.sys file as part of a complete Windows system, but you will require them when booting into DOS. It is quite possible to end up in the position of having an unusable system because you can't load the CD-Rom drivers from the CD-Rom that has them on.

Backing up your work files

If you want to dual boot then it is strongly recommended that you back up all of your work files. You have a number of options here depending on what devices you have installed:

- floppy drive
- zip drive
- CD writer
- network connection.

The last two are obviously the quickest and easiest way of backing these files up.

Hard disks background

Hard disks have a structure imposed upon them by a combination of a disk partitioning program and a formatting program. The structure will vary with the operating system. In the context of DOS and Windows the following will be found:

- FAT
- The original PC file system. Actually stands for File Allocation Table. Can be used from DOS, Windows 3.x, Windows 95, Windows NT and OS/2.
- FAT16
- A proprietary Microsoft file system to overcome the limitations of the original FAT system.
- FAT32
- This uses 32-bit file allocation table entries. Came in with Windows 95 OSR2. Can be used with Windows 98 and 2000.
- NTFS
- Windows NT only.

A disk can be organized into partitions, with both primary and extended partitions and one or more logical drives.

FDISK

FDISK is a program that will provide partition and logical drive information about your hard drives. You can run the program from a DOS session. The following screen shots take you through using FDISK to obtain information about how your hard drive is partitioned and what logical drives there are. The key concepts are:

- firstly to organize a disk drive into partitions
- secondly to organize the disk into logical drives within a partition.

It is recommended that you run this program to gain some familiarity with the set up of your own system. The following screen shots are taken from a PC with two hard disks and show clearly the two points about breaking a disk down into one or more partitions and one or more logical drives with these partitions.

FDISK opening screen

This is the FDISK opening screen.

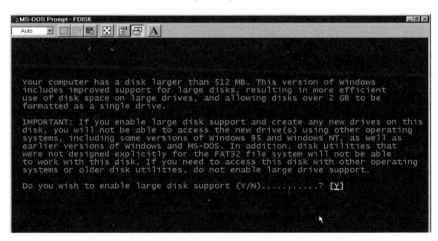

We choose enable large disk support.

FDISK main menu options

This brings up the FDISK main menu.

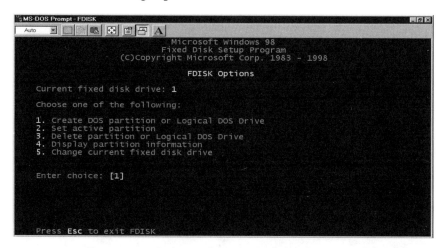

Now we are interested in 4: Display partition information.

FDISK display partition and logical drive information

This brings up the following screen.

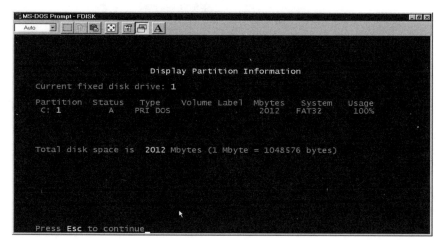

This disk only has one partition.

Change current disk drive

Press [ESC] and then choose 5 to change the current disk drive. This generates the following screen.

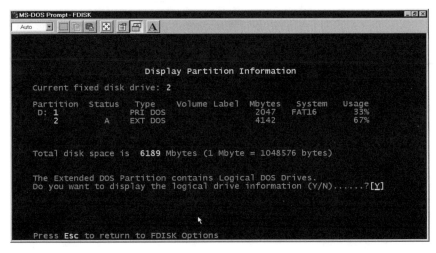

Choose 2 and this will bring up the following screen.

This disk has two partitions.

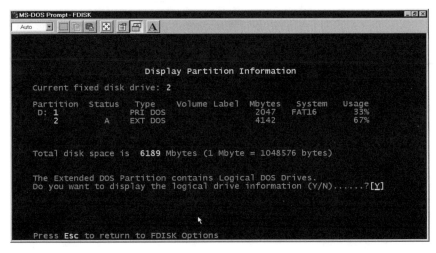

What type of Linux installation?

In Chapter 2 we looked at several installation options. The exact steps you need to take will depend on what kind of installation you are making.

Single booting

This is the easiest. All you need to do is delete all partitions and logical disk drives. The whole of the hard drive can then be used for the Linux installation. The DOS/Windows FDISK program is very easy to use and you can use that to partition the disk ready for the Linux install. Alternatively you can use the disk partitioning software that comes with the version of Linux you have. Booting Linux from the hard drive is the fastest and most reliable. You should also create one or more boot floppies during the Linux installation. In the event of a disk crash you can boot and repair the hard drive.

Dual booting

This provides the best of both worlds. You can boot into both Windows and Linux. You have a number of options here depending on your BIOS and network card. You will have the option of one or more of the following:

- floppy disk boot
- hard disk boot
- CD-Rom boot
- network boot.

The first two are found on older systems, the third will be an option on newer systems and the fourth will be an option with certain network cards.

Running from a CD

A version of SuSe Linux is available which boots from the CD and does a minimal install on your hard drive without requiring partitioning. Linux runs from the CD. This is obviously not as fast as a hard disk install but does run perfectly adequately on a Pentium PII 350 with 192Mb of memory. It requires about 150Mb of hard disk space.

Installing without partitioning

Red Hat provide the option of installing without partitioning. If you don't want to get into the intricacies of partitioning then this is an easy option.

Installing on a separate hard disk

If you have a spare drive then you can dedicate the whole of this drive to Linux. You have Windows on one and Linux on the others and they don't interact with one another.

Installing on a disk that has DOS and Windows

You will need to free up all of a partition for the Linux install. This will probably involve one or more of the following:

- removing software from the proposed Linux partition
- reinstalling this software on the DOS/Windows partition if required
- deleting or moving all work files from the proposed Linux partition.

Third party software can be used to help out here and Powerquest market a product called Partition Magic that simplifies the above process a lot. It supports both Windows and Linux partitions.

SuSe and Red Hat provide a utility called fips that is a program that can resize FAT partitions. It is in the DOSutils directory on the SuSe and Red Hat CDs.

The next section provides some background to partitioning so that you can decide for yourself which type of installation is best for you.

Partitions and the Linux file system

On a DOS and Windows system you will have one or more hard drives. Each hard drive can have one or more partitions and one or more logical drives. These drives are called C:, D:, E:, etc. You access files on these drives through the drive name, a directory structure and the file name.

On a Linux system you have similar functionality, but instead of accessing files through the drive name you will access files through a device name, mount point and directory structure and file name. This is best illustrated with an example taken from a Linux system. The following output is obtained by typing

- df -k

on a SuSe Linux system. df is a program that reports information on the file system disk space usage.

Filesystem	1k-blocks	Used	Available	Use%	Mounted on
/dev/hda6	1320016	1188492	63388	95%	/
/dev/hda5	3745	1378	2167	39%	/boot
/dev/hdc	653632	653632	0	100%	/cdrom

This is a system with one hard drive and one CD drive.

Looking at the Filesystem column, hda refers to the hard drive and hdc refers to the CD drive. The hard drive has two visible partitions, hda5 and hda6. Under DOS, typing

- dir c:\

would list all of the files and directories on the root of that drive.

Under Linux, typing

- ls /

would provide the same type of information. Note the use of the \ character under DOS and / under Linux.

During the installation procedure at least the following three partitions will need to be made:

- swap
- /boot
- / or root – the rest.

From the use of the df command above we see that the swap partition is not shown. We will look at each in more depth.

swap

No matter how much physical memory you have you will eventually require more than you have. It is in this case that an operating system will "swap" out to disk processes or pages of memory that aren't being used to enable this memory to used by another process. A common guideline is to create a swap file equal in size to your physical memory.

/boot

You will need to create a small partition to enable Linux to boot when you power the system up. This partition is less than 16Mb.

/

Finally you need a partition for the Linux operating system and user space.

I've found the following file sizes with several of the installations I've made:

- swap – 64Mb
- /boot – 16Mb
- / – the rest of the hard disk.

You may be lucky and find that the installation process does the above for you or you may find that you actually have to set the above.

In addition to partitioning the disk you need to define mount points.

The main difference between DOS and Linux is that each partition is used to form part of the storage necessary to support a single set of files and directories. This is done by associating a partition with a directory through a process known as mounting. Mounting a partition makes its storage available starting at the specified directory (known as a mount point).

Both Red Hat and SuSe offer programs to help out here. It shouldn't be necessary to use the raw Linux FDISK partition program.

Printing documentation prior to the install

If you've gone for the option of installing from a non-boxed CD set then I would recommend printing out some of the documentation prior to the install.

On a Red Hat 6.2 set the documentation can be found in HTML format in three directories under the doc directory.

They are

- gsg – Getting Started Guide
- install-guide – Installation Guide
- ref-guide – Reference Guide.

They can also be found in Adobe Acrobat Portable Document Format (PDF) at Red Hat's site. I would recommend getting hold of the PDF versions for printing purposes.

- Getting Started Guide – 362 pages
- Installation Guide – 99 pages
- Reference Guide – 375 pages.

Even if you buy one of the boxed Red Hat version 7 sets then you should consider printing this documentation. They provide much more information than the printed books that come with the distributions.

The SuSe 6.4 single evaluation CD has the documentation in the

- docu

directory.

The English version of the printed book that you get with the full boxed set is called

- Book-en.pdf

and is over 530 pages.

The SuSE 7 boxed sets also provide PDF versions. If you install on more than one machine then printing copies for each machine helps a lot.

Boot floppy

If you can't boot from your CD then you will need a boot floppy. The boxed sets come with a boot floppy. If you've gone for one of the other options then you will need to create a boot floppy using the rawrite utility.

This can be found in the

- DOSutils\rawrite

directory on the SuSe 6.4 distribution and under

- DOSutils

under Red Hat 6.2.

You should find a Word document with the rawrite instructions. Follow the instructions and insert the floppy.

TCP/IP and networking

If the machines are to be networked then you will need to have some information available prior to starting the installation. It is assumed that you have an Ethernet card installed. Each machine on the network will need an IP address to be able to communicate with other networked systems.

Ethernet card MAC address.

Each Ethernet card has a unique address. This is called a MAC address. The following is a MAC address taken from a 3COM 3c509 card.

● 00;A0:24:47:F3:CD

You probably won't need to know anything about MAC addresses if you have a network at home. You will if you are part of a wider network. The network support people will generally keep a database of MAC addresses and corresponding IP addresses.

IP address and other network information

There are several classes of networks:

● Class A – range 1.0.0.0 through 127.0.0.0
  ○ approximately 1.6 million hosts.
● Class B – range 128.0.0.0 through 191.255.0.0
  ○ 16065 networks with 65534 hosts.
● Class C – range 192.0.0.0 through 223.255.255.0
  ○ approximately 2 million networks with up to 254 hosts.
● Numbers in the range 224 through 239
  ○ multicast
● Over 239
  ○ reserved.

You can assign the following if you are using a local network.

- Class A – 10.0.0.0 through 10.255.255.255
- Class B – 172.16.0.0 through 172.31.255.255
- Class C – 192.168.0.0 through 192.168.255.255.

You can't use some IP addresses because they are used by the network.

If you are communicating directly to the Internet then you will need to be assigned a valid IP address. Contact your local network administrator. You will require one or more of the following:

- hostname – the name of your system
- IP address – its address
- subnet mask – the subnet mask
- default gateway – the default gateway for routing
- broadcast address
- DNS address – domain name servers

depending on your exact requirements.

We will cover the above in more detail in the chapter on networking.

The names of the program to run will depend on which version of Windows you have:
- Windows 95
  - winipcfg
- Windows 98
  - winipcfg
- Windows NT
  - ipconfig.

Sample output from both of them is given opposite.

```
IP Configuration                                    _ □ ×
┌Host Information──────────────────────────────────────┐
│              Host Name    magnolia.cc.kcl.ac.uk      │
│            DNS Servers    137.73.2.8            ...   │
│             Node Type     Hybrid                     │
│        NetBIOS Scope Id                              │
│       IP Routing Enabled  ☐    WINS Proxy Enabled ☐  │
│  NetBIOS Resolution Uses DNS ✓                       │
├Ethernet Adapter Information──────────────────────────┤
│                         ELNK3 Ethernet Adapter    ▾  │
│        Adapter Address    00-20-AF-F2-B3-EA          │
│             IP Address    137.73.204.22              │
│            Subnet Mask    255.255.255.0              │
│        Default Gateway    137.73.204.1               │
│            DHCP Server    137.73.173.4               │
│     Primary WINS Server   137.73.254.250             │
│   Secondary WINS Server   137.73.254.246             │
│         Lease Obtained    Mon Jan 8 01 09:38:57      │
│          Lease Expires    Mon Jan 8 01 21:38:57      │
└──────────────────────────────────────────────────────┘
  [  OK  ]  [ Release ]  [ Renew ]  [ Release All ]  [ Renew All ]
```

ipconfig/all Windows NT 4 Server

```
Windows NT IP Configuration
   Host Name . . . . . . . . . : pc102.cc.kcl.ac.uk
   DNS Servers . . . . . . . . : 137.73.2.5
   Node Type . . . . . . . . . : Broadcast
   NetBIOS Scope ID . . . . . . :
   IP Routing Enabled . . . . . : No
   WINS Proxy Enabled . . . . . : No
   NetBIOS Resolution Uses DNS. : Yes
Ethernet adapter E190x1:
   Description . . . . . . . . : 3Com 3C90x Ethernet Adapter
   Physical Address . . . . . . : 00-50-DA-DF-17-6E
   DHCP Enabled . . . . . . . . : No
   IP Address. . . . . . . . . : 137.73.36.102
   Subnet Mask . . . . . . . . : 255.255.254.0
   Default Gateway . . . . . . : 137.73.16.30
```

Final note

Don't panic! There is a lot to assimilate.

Bibliography

The actual printed documentation you get with your system varies enormously from supplier to supplier. If you need help on the DOS and Windows side the on-line help may be adequate.

DOS

Pure DOS books are getting rarer. You best bet is probably in a second-hand book shop or the Internet. Here are some websites:

- http://www.salokin.demon.co.uk/DOS_links.htm
- http://www.theusefulsite.com/DOS_links.htm
- http://www.theusefulsite.com/index.html
- http://www.theusefulsite.com/win_links.htm
- http://www.theusefulsite.com/DOS.htm

to start with.

Windows

One that you might find useful is:

O'Reilly T., Mott T. & Glenn W., *Windows 98 in a Nutshell*, O'Reilly.

It should also be useful if you have a Windows 95 system. I've not found anything at this time to recommend on Windows ME.

If you need more in-depth technical information then the Microsoft Press Windows Resource Kit Series is worth a look. There are editions for each version of Windows.

Linux

Look at the READMEs and documentation that came with your CDs. Some are available from the supplier's website.

Networking

Hunt C., *TCP/IP Network Administration*, O'Reilly

- I found this provided most of what I needed to know to network the systems I work with effectively.

Chapter 4

Installing Linux

The aim of this chapter is to look at actually installing Linux. There
is coverage of a number of ways of doing the installation. The set up
of the windowing side is left to the next chapter.

The examples in this chapter provide coverage of some of the
common ways of installing and running Linux. With each
example there are details of what happened during the
installation procedure. What is common to all of the
following is:

- The preparation of DOS and Windows boot floppies so
  that if the installation failed it would be possible to
  reboot the machine and reinstall DOS and Windows.
- Any hardware manuals that came with the system were
  at hand.
- A printout of the actual hardware in the system was
  available in case there were any problems during the install
  with hardware detection and set up by Linux. Details of
  how to obtain this are given in the previous chapter.
- A boot floppy or CD to start the Linux install.
- The printed manuals that came with the distribution or
  printed copies of the documentation for that distribution. The latter is either on the CDs or is available at
  the SuSE or Red Hat websites. Details are given in the
  previous chapter. If you have another machine nearby
  then you can be tree-friendly and browse the documentation on-line. Most is available as PDF or HTML.
- A notebook to document what you actually did and log
  any messages generated during the install.
- The set up of a log-in account and root account.

What is also common to all examples is to follow the
instructions that appear during the install. Don't panic if you
are not sure about any of the choices. Have a look to see if
any help is available at each stage. If not, have a look at the
manuals and documentation that you have available. A large
part of computing involves RTFM or Read The Fabulous
Manual. The first time I heard this expression was at Imperial
College whilst phoning technical support for one of the
major hardware manufacturers. A voice in the background
said that it was an RTFM problem! You are installing Linux

for the first time and there is a lot of technical information to assimilate.

During each installation you will also have to choose the following:

- language to use
- keyboard
- mouse – this should be automatic
- monitor
- graphics card.

These are common to most installations. The set up of the monitor and graphics card is covered again in more depth in the next chapter on X-Windows, windows managers and initial start-up. You may also have to set up one or more of the following depending on the exact hardware you have:

- Ethernet card
- printer
- scanner
- modem.

You should have the details of all of the above available for the install.

Single booting at home, local area network, booting from /boot

This system is relatively old, with a Pentium P75 and 32Mb of memory. It has a 2Gb hard drive and a CD-Rom.

FDISK had been used under DOS to repartition the disk and a minimal DOS system installed on the hard drive. This system can't boot from the CD-Rom so rawrite was used to create a boot floppy. The CD that came with the distribution was inserted into the CD drive and the boot floppy inserted and the system rebooted and the installation started.

This installation was done using the SuSe 6.4 boxed set distribution. As the system had 32Mb of memory the text-based install was followed. SuSe call this YaST – Yet another Setup Tool. The defaults offered were generally chosen. The first problem during this install came with the mouse. The initial detection worked, but problems were encountered during the X-Windows set up. It was necessary to experiment with several types of mouse before one was found that worked reliably. The second problem came with the Compuadd monitor. This was a monitor from an old 33Mhz 80486 system. There were no manuals and it wasn't possible to get the monitor working properly with X-Windows under Linux.

Fortunately I had another old 80486-based Gateway system that I was setting up for the charitable organization my wife worked for. I swapped the monitors over and did the Linux install a second time. This worked.

This system is part of a local network at home. The other systems used the following IP addresses

- 10.0.0.1
- 10.0.0.2

The SuSe system was given

- 10.0.0.4

as an IP address.

I followed the guidelines in the Hunt book on subnet mask and chose

- 255.255.255.0

All machines on the same physical network segment must have the same subnet mask.

Dual boot system at home, local area network, booting from CD

This system is a Pentium PII 350 with 192Mb of memory and runs Windows 98. It's the machine that my kids have their games on. This system can boot from the CD and the BIOS was entered and the boot sequence altered to boot from CD. The single SuSe 7 evaluation CD was used. This system has several peripherals including scanner, printer and web camera. Make sure that you switch on all of your peripherals before starting the install. This allows the set-up and detection software to determine your exact system configuration and hopefully let you set them all up. It has a PCI modem and this was not set up automatically during the install. SuSe provide details of how to do this at a later stage.

The install created a number of files on the C drive, about 150Mb in all. Given the processor speed, memory and speed of the CD drive the performance of this type of install is quite respectable.

When you've finished using Linux you restart the system, enter the BIOS settings, make the boot sequence floppy and hard drive, and the system will then restart in Windows.

Dual boot system at home, local area network, booting from /boot

This is a Cyrix system with two hard drives of 2Gb and 6Gb capacity. The disks had been organized as

- disk 1 – one partition, C drive
- disk 2 – two partitions, with D on the first partition and E,F and G in the extended partition.

This system was inherited from a friend when he went to work in the USA. It had been built from components and there had always been problems getting the system to work reliably. During the installation of the network card under Windows 95, for example, it proved impossible to get the network card, graphics card and sound card to work simultaneously. In the end I bought a PCI-based sound card.

There has also been a lot of software installation and removal as it was my production system for some time and the children tried out a lot of games on it.

The second disk was set up to install and run Linux. Software installed on E, F or G drive was removed. Files from D E and F were either backed up or deleted. The drives in the extended partition on the second disk were made available for Linux. FDISK was used to wipe out the three drives in the extended partition. The C and D drives were kept for DOS and Windows 95. After this had been done the system became very slow to boot, and would hang from time to time. I decided to proceed with the installation anyway. If the system became completely unusable I was prepared to reinstall DOS and Windows and start again.

SuSe Linux 7 Professional was used. The boot floppy and first CD were inserted into their respective drives and the system rebooted. The installation instructions were followed and the first thing of interest with this install is the requirement to partition the drives.

The set-up software identified

- /dev/hda
- /dev/hdc

as being available for the install. hda is the C drive and hdc is D, E, F and G. The install offered

- hdc1
- hdc2
- hdc5
- hdc6
- hdc7

as being available. hdc1 is the D drive and is the DOS first partition. hdc2 is the extended partition which is made up of hdc5, hdc6 and hdc7.

The SuSE 7.0 partitioning software was used. Firstly the three partitions set aside for Linux were deleted. The original sizes were not suitable for the Linux install. Three new partitions were then created. The first was set aside for booting from. Remember this partition has to be less than 16Mb. The second was set aside for Linux. The third was about 196Mb and set aside for the swap file. I used a calculator to go between the cylinder information offered by the partitioning software and the sizes in Mb and Gb.

After completing the partitioning of the disk the partitions set aside for Linux and booting have to be mounted. The mount points are

- / for the Linux system
- /boot for the boot partition.

The installation takes care of the swap file set-up for you.

The file systems are then created and you are offered a range of SuSe installs. I found this part of the installation a little quirky. It took a couple of attempts before I successfully got things set up correctly.

The next part offers you the install option. Choosing

- Load configuration

provides a number of different types of installation. I chose SuSe Default system with office and pressing the space bar selects the one you want. The install then starts in earnest.

When complete you save the configuration and exit via the main menu. There was no kernel option for the Cyrix processor. The generic x386, x486 was chosen.

The next stage of the installation took place. This involves setting up

- the Ethernet connection
- mouse
- modem.

I chose to install LiLo in the hard disk master boot record. The system was then rebooted and the system hung.

The system was rebooted into Windows safe mode and FDISK was used to wipe out the C and D drives. Windows was reinstalled from scratch, the rest of the software reinstalled and the Linux installation redone, now choosing boot from floppy. Take care to remove the set-up floppy. The floppy isn't write protected and I overwrote it. A quick chat with the SuSe technical support people enabled me to locate the image file (called bootdisk) and I used rawrite to recreate the set-up disk. As floppies fail you are recommended to create two boot floppies. This worked! The next problem that arose concerned setting up the keyboard under the X-Windows system and with the graphics card. This is a Videologic GrafixStar 600. Support for this graphics card is not part of the standard installation and it is necessary to add support for this card at a later stage. The keyboard has 105 keys and there are keyboard mapping problems with the | character – the ~ character generates the | character.

At a later stage I installed loadlin and then had the option of doing a boot off the C drive. This involves the following:

- Starting the system in Windows mode and copying the loadlin files from the first SuSe CD. They are in the \DOSutils\loadlin directory. They were copied into the directory \loadlin on the C drive.

- Copying the kernel from /boot into the \loadlin directory on the C drive. This was done using the mcopy utility provided on the SuSe system. This can write DOS-format floppies. After changing to /boot the command mcopy vmlinuz a: will copy the file onto the floppy disk.

- Modify the linux.bat file to reflect the set-up on this system. The actual file is shown later.

- Run linux.bat. If you are not in DOS real mode the system will reboot in this mode and start up Linux.

You can create a keyboard short cut to run linux.bat if you want.

This is the sample file:

```
rem  Sample DOS batch file to boot Linux.
rem  First, ensure any unwritten disk buffers are flushed:
     smartdrv /C
rem  Start the LOADLIN process:
     c:\loadlin\loadlin
     c:\loadlin\vmlinuz
     root=/dev/hdc6
     ro
     vga=3
```

The key points are:

- c:\loadlin\vmlinuz

which is the Linux kernel and

- root=/dev/hdc6

which is the root partition on this system. 'ro' means mount the file system as read only. I can't find out what the last option does.

They keyboard mapping problem under X-Windows is looked at in a later chapter.

Partitionless install

With Red Hat 7 comes the possibility of a partitionless installation. All you require is a disk that has a formatted DOS (FAT) file system with sufficient space. This is an attractive option if you a reasonable specification machine and don't want to go to the trouble of making an empty partition.

This was done using the Pentium PII 350 at home. In fact this system is therefore a triple boot system, depending on whether I boot from floppy (Red Hat), local hard disk (Windows 98) or CD (SuSe).

This involves booting from the Red Hat 7 floppy or from the CD and following the instructions. At the section where you are asked about partitioning you highlight the DOS partition you want to make root or /. You then click on the [Edit] button and just type in / as the mount point. You then follow the rest of the instructions.

The install incorrectly identified both the monitor and graphics card. Selecting the correct ones and proceeding eventually left the system in an unusable state. The next screen in the installation process was garbage.

I rebooted and repeated the install. The above happened again.

I contacted Red Hat via their web pages and they got back several days later and recommended trying again but this time not setting up X-Windows. I tried to do this using the graphical install. The install eventually failed with an error message that there was probably a bug in the installation set-up and to contact Red Hat with details. This involved putting a blank floppy in the drive for the error report. I did this but nothing was written to the floppy.

I tried the installation again choosing text-based install. The graphics card was again incorrectly identified but I did eventually end up with a complete usable installed system. Interestingly enough the monitor was identified correctly during this install. The system boots from a floppy.

Single boot system at work, network connected, booting from /boot

Three Pentium P75s with 32Mb of memory were set up in this way. The systems are nominally identical.

Two systems were set up in this way using the Red Hat 6.2 cheap CD distribution. I work with a numerical analyst and we share the program language teaching and support at King's. We have an educational licence for a high-performance numerical library for several platforms including both g77 and NAG f95 compilers under Linux. Details of how to install this library are an example in the chapter on installing third party software.

The set up of both these systems was straightforward. There were network problems with one of the systems that were resolved with the replacement of the 3Com 3C509 card.

A third system was set up using the SuSe 6.4 distribution. This was straightforward. The only problem occurred with the network set up. It was not possible to access the external network. Curiously the machine could be seen by other machines on the network using ping. We will cover this utility (which is one of the Unix commands) in a later chapter.

One of our network team tested out the various network set-ups. The cable was the cause of the problem.

The cable was replaced. It was found that a system reboot was required to make the network set up to function.

All three systems were probed relatively quickly after being connected to the network and we will look in a subsequent chapter at what can be done to make systems like this more secure.

Dual boot system at work, network connected, LiLo

The Red Hat 7 Deluxe edition was used for this installation. This system is a Pentium P120 with 64Mb of memory. Two drives are installed. The first is 2.6Gb. The second hard drive was 10Gb, and 4Gb was set aside for DOS and Windows with the other 6Gb for Linux. Windows 95 and Windows NT Workstation are installed.

The system could not boot from CD so the Red Hat boot disk was used. A workstation installation was chosen. The installation process set the system up as dual bootable automatically and it was not necessary to do any partitioning.

Monitor and graphics card

The monitor can be driven at a range of horizontal and vertical refresh rates. The ranges will be specific to the monitor. Horizontal refresh rates are in kHz and vertical refresh rates are in Hz.

Hopefully the installation will automatically detect both the graphics card and monitor. If not you will need to have a look at the options presented. During the above installs the monitor and graphics card had to be set explicitly on a couple of occasions. Under SuSe Linux the drivers for the VideoLogic graphics card were not installed. They had to be explicitly added later. This is covered in a later chapter.

The Compuadd monitor could not be successfully set up, and fortunately there was a Gateway monitor that was supported and worked.

You've also seen that the partitionless install had problems with identifying the graphics card and monitor.

You can damage the monitor if it is driven at higher refresh rates than it can support. Err on the side of caution.

Summary

The above has shown that the ease of installation varies quite widely. If anything goes wrong you need to be patient. The key is the documentation. The information you require is probably there but it is not necessarily that easy to find. This is to be expected to a certain extent as Linux is a new operating system to you and there is a lot to get on top of. The DOS and Windows terminology is obviously different from the Unix and Linux terminology.

Security and Linux

Any computer system connected to a network is liable to be hacked. The only safe system is one that is not network connected, and is in a locked room. Linux is no exception.

The experience at King's with Linux (in reality any of our network-connected systems) is that our systems are probed and attempts made to hack relatively quickly after the systems are network connected. The mainstream Linux distributions are relatively open. Work has to be done by you to tighten up the security to prevent the system being used to attack other systems.

We will look at this issue in more depth in a later chapter.

Bibliography

SuSe

The 6.4 release boxed set came with

- Installation Guide
- Handbook ~ 500 pages.

The Handbook is also available on the CD in the docu directory.

The SuSe 6.4 evaluation CD comes with

- Handbook ~ 530 pages

in the docu directory.

The 7.0 release boxed set comes with

- Installation Guide
- Configuration Guide
- Applications Guide
- Handbook ~ 600 pages.

The SuSe 7 evaluation CD comes without any printed manual and there is no PDF version of the handbook on the CD. Versions can be found at the SuSe site. I found them in:

- ftp://ftp.suse.com/pub/suse/i386/7.0/docu/

If you have this version then I would download a copy. It will make using the system much easier and give you a better feel for the complete version.

Red Hat

One Red Hat 6.2 cheap CD set comes with the

- Installation Guide
- Getting Started Guide
- Reference Guide

as HTML. There were no PDF versions of the documentation. The HTML is fine for using whilst at the machine but can't be printed easily like the PDF versions.

The Red Hat 7 Standard Edition comes with

- Installation Guide
- Getting Started Guide.

The Red Hat 7.0 Deluxe boxed set comes with

- Installation Guide
- Getting Started Guide.

So, effectively, there are the following sources of information:

- on-line – HTML
- on-line – PDF
- paper – books
- paper – printed copies of the on-line material in HTML format. This source can generally only be printed in small sections.
- paper – printed copies of the PDF versions. This can be printed in one go.

You need to consider your own working methods. Some people find the on-line material adequate, others like a book or paper copy to work with. The costs and speed of your printers are also a factor to consider.

Chapter

5

Linux and Windows

This chapter looks at what windowing options are available with Linux. We will look at

- X-Windows
- XFree86
- choosing a windows manager
- starting up our system with a windows manager.

We start first with a little history.

X-Windows and XFree86

The X-Windows system is the de facto standard graphical user interface for Unix systems. The original X-Windows was developed by Digital Equipment Corporation (DEC, now Compaq) and Project Athena at Massachusetts Institute of Technology (MIT).

XFree86 is a free X server implementation for the PC. It was developed by a number of people who founded the XFree86 team in 1992. This subsequently led to the foundation of the XFree86 Project in 1994. They continue with research and development of the system.

Simplistically the X-Windows system or X server provides the following services

- communicates with the graphics card
- handles drawing dots, lines, etc. on the screen
- manages the services on the local host.

A windows manager sits on top of this and actually provides the user interface.

Windows managers

There are a number of windows managers for Unix. Three commonly available ones are:

- KDE – The K Desktop Environment which is standard with SuSe Linux
- Gnome – The GNU Network Object Model Environment which is the default with a Red Hat distribution
- CDE – The Common Desktop Environment, which is a commercial product.

We will cover them in turn. First we need to look at a few fundamentals that are common to most windowing systems.

Some basics

We will start by looking at a screenshot from a system running Microsoft Windows. The following is taken from one running Windows 98.

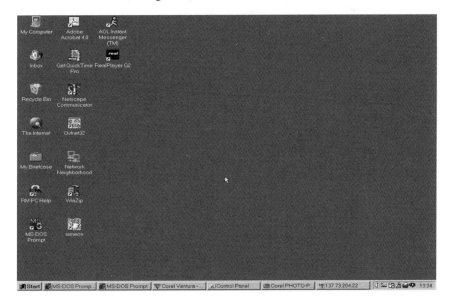

When using a PC your interface to the system will generally consist of a screen made up of a background, a bar at the bottom and several icons on the left-hand side. The bar at the bottom will have a button on the left that has the Windows flag and Start on it. Pressing this button will then bring up several more choices.

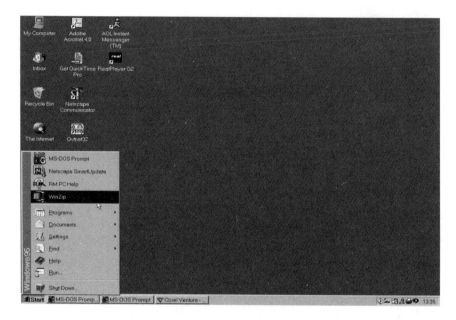

When an application runs you will have three buttons at the
top right that minimize, maximize and terminate the
application. The minimized application can be accessed by
clicking on the application button that appears on the bar at
the bottom.

The left-hand side of the desktop will have a mixture of icons that can be used to start an application - sometimes called launching it - and folders. Folders correspond to directories.

Double click versus single click

Microsoft Windows activates many things with two quick clicks. Linux does it with one click. If nothing appears to happen after clicking be patient, especially on less powerful systems.

Logging on for the first time

Either the system will have set itself up to drop straight into one of the windows managers or you will need to do that from the terminal session. Typing

- startx

will normally bring up your windows manager. We'll look at the KDE and Gnome windows managers now.

Both the SuSe and Red Hat sites have introductory on-line documentation. The SuSe start page is

- http://www.suse.com/en/linux/index.html

but I've found the following more useful

- http://www.suse.com/en/linux/about/index.html

The Red Hat home page is

- http://www.redhat.com/apps/support/

and the following is the home page for the Getting Started Guide:

- http://www.redhat.com/support/manuals/RHL-6.2-Manual/getting-started-guide/

A PDF version of this file can also be found and printed. That home page is

* http://www.redhat.com/support/manuals/

KDE

This is the default under SuSe. It is an option with Red Hat. The opening screen should be similar to that shown below.

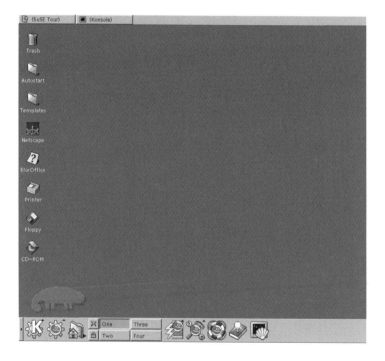

The set up is similar to Microsoft Windows. The start button is in the same place. Don't worry if things are a bit confusing. This panel also has several launch buttons. Clicking on them will start an application. Move the mouse over each button in turn. A little box will appear providing you with a text message that hopefully gives you some idea as to what will happen if you click on that button.

This desktop has a task bar at the top. This has details of all running programs. This makes it very easy to switch between them.

The behaviour of the KDE is relatively slow on the P75 systems with 32Mb of memory. Other windows managers are provided on the SuSe disks and if you have a system like the above then it might be better to install a less resource-hungry desktop. It is quite acceptable on the Cyrix system with 48Mb of memory.

KDE help

There is extensive help available on how to use the KDE under both SuSe and Red Hat.

Under SuSe there is an icon on the bottom panel with book and light bulb. Clicking on this will bring up a help Window. The help is organized into the following sections:

- Welcome to the K Desktop Environment
  - What is the K Desktop Environment?
  - Contacting the KDE Project
  - Supporting the KDE Project
- KDE Help Contents
  - KDE application help index
  - System man page contents
  - System GNU info contents
  - Search for Keyword
- Getting the most out of KDE
  - A Quick Start Guide to the Desktop
  - Desktop Panel
  - Control Center
  - File Manager
  - Window Manager.

It is recommended that you explore this help system to gain some familiarity with how the KDE is organized and what is has to offer.

Multiple desktops

The KDE will also provide you with the option of working with multiple desktops. These are available via the buttons labelled

- One
- Two
- Three
- Four

on the panel at the bottom.

Tasks running

A task bar will show what you are running. Under SuSe 6.4 this is at the bottom. Under SuSe 7 it is at the top. If you minimize a task you can easily restart it by clicking on the appropriate button.

Drag and drop

The KDE supports drag and drop. This means that you can move files between

- the file system
- CD drive
- floppy drive

using the file manager.

Gnome

Gnome is the default with Red Hat. However the install will offer two desktop environments, Gnome and KDE. You can decide to install both. The Red Hat opening desktop is shown below.

The set-up is similar to Microsoft Windows. The Start button is in the same place. Don't worry if things are a bit confusing. This panel also has several launch buttons. Clicking on them will start an application. Move the mouse over each button in turn. A little box will appear providing you with a text message that hopefully gives you some idea as to what will happen if you click on that button.

Gnome on-line help

There is extensive on-line help on how to use the Gnome desktop environment. There is an icon on the bottom panel with a bubble and question mark. Clicking on this will bring up a window with the Gnome help. You will find information on:

- Gnome User Guide
- Man pages
- Info pages
- Gnome documents.

Take the time to actually explore what is available and see what Gnome has to offer.

The Gnome home page is:

- http://www.gnome.org/

Gnome user guide address is:

- http://www.labs.redhat.com/gug/users-guide/

Multiple desktops

Gnome will also provide you with the option of working with multiple desktops. These are available via the buttons on the right of the panel at the bottom.

Tasks running

This is shown by buttons on the panel at the bottom. If you minimize a task you can easily restart it by clicking on the appropriate button.

Drag and drop

Gnome supports drag and drop. This means that you can move files between

- the file system
- CD drive
- floppy drive

using the file manager.

Summary

It is necessary to take the time to try using the windowing system that comes with your distribution. They are similar and offer much the same functionality as Microsoft Windows, which is probably what you are most familiar with.

Bibliography

There are typically three choices for further information. The first is whatever printed documentation came the distribution you have, the second is the on-line help that comes with your distribution and the third is what is available on the Internet.

KDE home page

Their home page is:

- http://www.kde.org/

Gnome home page

Their home page is:

- http://www.gnome.org/

CDE home page

The home page for the Opengroup is

- http://www.opengroup.org/

and their desktop home page is:

- http://www.opengroup.org/desktop/

Chapter 6

Basic Unix

The aim of this chapter is to provide coverage of a small set of Unix commands, literally just enough to get you started.

This chapter looks at a small set of Unix commands. You need to become familiar with using Unix from the command line. Whilst a graphical user interface can be very productive, some of the real power of Unix comes from the rich set of commands that are available and the way that you can use them to automate much that you do. We will come back to this in a later chapter.

There is also brief coverage of the editors that are available.

Command examples

The syntax of a command is

- command options arguments

and we will look at examples of each of the above.

Command on its own

- ls

This command lists the contents of the current directory. The following is some sample output from a Red Hat 7 system.

```
Desktop          gnomerpm01.png   linuxconf05.png   redhat704.ps
boot_floppy      gnomerpm01.ps    linuxconf05.ps    redhat705.ps
core             gnomerpm02.bmp   linuxconf10.bmp   redhat_bin.txt
gateway          gnomerpm02.gif   linuxconf10.gif   redhat_sbin.txt
gnome01.bmp      gnomerpm02.png   linuxconf10.png   redhat_usr_bin.txt
gnome01.gif      gnomerpm02.ps    linuxconf10.ps    redhat_usr_sbin.txt
gnome01.jpg      linuxconf01.png  ls.txt            snapshot001.bmp
gnome01.png      linuxconf02.png  lspci.root        snapshot001.gif
gnome01.ps       linuxconf05.bmp  lspci.v           snapshot001.png
gnomerpm01.bmp   linuxconf05.gif  nsmail            snapshot001.xbm
gnomerpm01.gif   linuxconf05.jpg  redhat701.ps      z.z
```

The number of columns will depend on the length of the file names.

Command with single option

- ls -l

  The -l option changes the way the ls command works. This command produces a listing of the contents of the current directory in a long format.

```
total 40924
drwxr-xr-x 5 sttp1553 sttp1553    4096 Nov 20 21:18 Desktop
-rw-rw---- 1 sttp1553 sttp1553 1474560 Dec  9 11:05 boot_floppy
-rw------- 1 sttp1553 sttp1553 1708032 Dec 18 10:01 core
-rw-rw-r-- 1 sttp1553 sttp1553     491 Dec  8 18:34 gateway
-rw-rw-r-- 1 sttp1553 sttp1553 2359350 Dec 10 14:25 gnome01.bmp
-rw-rw-r-- 1 sttp1553 sttp1553  181256 Dec 10 14:25 gnome01.gif
-rw-rw-r-- 1 sttp1553 sttp1553       0 Dec 10 14:25 gnome01.jpg
-rw-rw-r-- 1 sttp1553 sttp1553   44105 Dec 10 14:25 gnome01.png
-rw-rw-r-- 1 sttp1553 sttp1553 4784316 Dec 10 14:26 gnome01.ps
-rw-rw-r-- 1 sttp1553 sttp1553  751518 Dec 10 14:29 nomerpm01.bmp
-rw-rw-r-- 1 sttp1553 sttp1553   12128 Dec 10 14:29 gnomerpm01.gif
-rw-rw-r-- 1 sttp1553 sttp1553    9868 Dec 10 14:29 gnomerpm01.png
-rw-rw-r-- 1 sttp1553 sttp1553 1525892 Dec 10 14:28 gnomerpm01.ps
-rw-rw-r-- 1 sttp1553 sttp1553 2187318 Dec 10 14:31 gnomerpm02.bmp
-rw-rw-r-- 1 sttp1553 sttp1553   91458 Dec 10 14:31 gnomerpm02.gif
-rw-rw-r-- 1 sttp1553 sttp1553   27707 Dec 10 14:31 gnomerpm02.png
-rw-rw-r-- 1 sttp1553 sttp1553 4435841 Dec 10 14:31 gnomerpm02.ps
-rw-rw-r-- 1 sttp1553 sttp1553    7392 Dec  9 10:44 linuxconf01.png
-rw-rw-r-- 1 sttp1553 sttp1553    9736 Dec  9 10:44 linuxconf02.png
-rw-rw-r-- 1 sttp1553 sttp1553  727366 Dec  9 10:48 linuxconf05.bmp
-rw-rw-r-- 1 sttp1553 sttp1553   14743 Dec  9 10:46 linuxconf05.gif
-rw-rw-r-- 1 sttp1553 sttp1553       0 Dec  9 10:48 linuxconf05.jpg
-rw-rw-r-- 1 sttp1553 sttp1553   13024 Dec  9 10:46 linuxconf05.png
-rw-rw-r-- 1 sttp1553 sttp1553 1477094 Dec  9 10:48 linuxconf05.ps
-rw-rw-r-- 1 sttp1553 sttp1553  727366 Dec  9 10:49 linuxconf10.bmp
-rw-rw-r-- 1 sttp1553 sttp1553   11870 Dec  9 10:49 linuxconf10.gif
-rw-rw-r-- 1 sttp1553 sttp1553   10697 Dec  9 10:49 linuxconf10.png
-rw-rw-r-- 1 sttp1553 sttp1553 1477094 Dec  9 10:49 linuxconf10.ps
-rw-rw-r-- 1 sttp1553 sttp1553   20712 Dec 18 13:29 lslaRredhat70.txt
-rw-rw-r-- 1 sttp1553 sttp1553    4733 Dec 18 13:26 lslaredhat70.txt
-rw-rw-r-- 1 sttp1553 sttp1553       0 Dec 18 13:41 lslredhat70.txt
-rw-rw-r-- 1 root root             2448 Dec  8 18:34 lspci.root
-rw-rw-r-- 1 sttp1553 sttp1553    2435 Dec  8 18:34 lspci.v
-rw-rw-r-- 1 sttp1553 sttp1553     715 Dec 18 13:25 lsredhat70.txt
drwx------ 2 sttp1553 sttp1553    4096 Nov 26 12:00 nsmail
-rw-rw-r-- 1 sttp1553 sttp1553 4784316 Nov 26 12:19 redhat701.ps
```

```
-rw-rw-r-- 1 sttp1553 sttp1553 4784316 Nov 26 12:29 redhat704.ps
-rw-rw-r-- 1 sttp1553 sttp1553 4784316 Nov 26 12:30 redhat705.ps
-rw-rw-r-- 1 sttp1553 sttp1553    5264 Dec 18 09:22 redhat_bin.txt
-rw-rw-r-- 1 sttp1553 sttp1553   10249 Dec 15 13:53 redhat_sbin.txt
-rw-rw-r-- 1 sttp1553 sttp1553  107204 Dec 18 09:23 redhat_usr_bin.txt
-rw-rw-r-- 1 sttp1553 sttp1553    9828 Dec 18 09:24 redhat_usr_sbin.txt
-rw-rw-r-- 1 sttp1553 sttp1553 2359350 Nov 26 14:04 snapshot001.bmp
-rw-rw-r-- 1 sttp1553 sttp1553  181309 Nov 26 14:04 snapshot001.gif
-rw-rw-r-- 1 sttp1553 sttp1553   44122 Nov 26 14:04 snapshot001.png
-rw-rw-r-- 1 sttp1553 sttp1553  504727 Nov 26 14:04 snapshot001.xbm
-rw-rw-r-- 1 root root                0 Nov 22 18:42 z.z
```

We will cover the meaning of the additional information in a later chapter when we look in more depth at files and file management.

The following is a simple variant. The additional option means list all files, including so-called hidden files.

- ls -la

```
total 40988
drwx------ 15 sttp1553 sttp1553    4096 Dec 18 13:26 .
drwxr-xr-x  3 root root            4096 Nov 20 21:18 ..
-rw-------  1 sttp1553 sttp1553     752 Dec 18 09:20 .ICEauthority
-rw-------  1 sttp1553 sttp1553     115 Dec 18 09:20 .Xauthority
-rw-------  1 sttp1553 sttp1553    1384 Dec 15 16:20 .bash_history
-rw-r--r--  1 sttp1553 sttp1553      24 Nov 20 21:18 .bash_logout
-rw-r--r--  1 sttp1553 sttp1553     230 Nov 20 21:18 .bash_profile
-rw-r--r--  1 sttp1553 sttp1553     124 Nov 20 21:18 .bashrc
drwx------  2 sttp1553 sttp1553    4096 Dec 8  16:28 .cddbslave
drwx------  4 sttp1553 sttp1553    4096 Dec 15 14:00 .ee
-rw-r--r--  1 sttp1553 sttp1553     688 Nov 20 21:18 .emacs
-rw-------  1 sttp1553 sttp1553      16 Nov 21 10:01 .esd_auth
drwxr-xr-x  6 sttp1553 sttp1553    4096 Dec 18 09:20 .gnome
drwxrwxr-x  3 sttp1553 sttp1553    4096 Dec 15 16:16 .gnome-desktop
drwxr-xr-x  2 sttp1553 sttp1553    4096 Nov 22 18:48 .gnome-help-browser
drwx------  2 sttp1553 sttp1553    4096 Dec 8  16:28 .gnome_private
drwxr-xr-x  3 sttp1553 sttp1553    4096 Nov 20 21:18 .kde
-rw-r--r--  1 sttp1553 sttp1553     365 Nov 26 14:05 .kderc
drwxrwxr-x  2 sttp1553 sttp1553    4096 Dec 15 15:50 .mc
drwxrwxr-x  5 sttp1553 sttp1553    4096 Nov 26 12:01 .netscape
drwxrwxr-x  3 sttp1553 sttp1553    4096 Nov 20 21:52 .sawfish
-rw-r--r--  1 sttp1553 sttp1553    3651 Nov 20 21:18 .screenrc
drwx------  3 sttp1553 sttp1553    4096 Nov 21 09:59 .xauth
-rw-------  1 sttp1553 sttp1553     481 Dec 18 11:59 .xsession-errors
drwxr-xr-x  5 sttp1553 sttp1553    4096 Nov 20 21:18 Desktop
```

```
-rw-rw----  1 sttp1553 sttp1553  1474560 Dec  9 11:05 boot_floppy
-rw-------  1 sttp1553 sttp1553  1708032 Dec 18 10:01 core
-rw-rw-r--  1 sttp1553 sttp1553      491 Dec  8 18:34 gateway
-rw-rw-r--  1 sttp1553 sttp1553  2359350 Dec 10 14:25 gnome01.bmp
-rw-rw-r--  1 sttp1553 sttp1553   181256 Dec 10 14:25 gnome01.gif
-rw-rw-r--  1 sttp1553 sttp1553        0 Dec 10 14:25 gnome01.jpg
-rw-rw-r--  1 sttp1553 sttp1553    44105 Dec 10 14:25 gnome01.png
-rw-rw-r--  1 sttp1553 sttp1553  4784316 Dec 10 14:26 gnome01.ps
-rw-rw-r--  1 sttp1553 sttp1553   751518 Dec 10 14:29 gnomerpm01.bmp
-rw-rw-r--  1 sttp1553 sttp1553    12128 Dec 10 14:29 gnomerpm01.gif
-rw-rw-r--  1 sttp1553 sttp1553     9868 Dec 10 14:29 gnomerpm01.png
-rw-rw-r--  1 sttp1553 sttp1553  1525892 Dec 10 14:28 gnomerpm01.ps
-rw-rw-r--  1 sttp1553 sttp1553  2187318 Dec 10 14:31 gnomerpm02.bmp
-rw-rw-r--  1 sttp1553 sttp1553    91458 Dec 10 14:31 gnomerpm02.gif
-rw-rw-r--  1 sttp1553 sttp1553    27707 Dec 10 14:31 gnomerpm02.png
-rw-rw-r--  1 sttp1553 sttp1553  4435841 Dec 10 14:31 gnomerpm02.ps
-rw-rw-r--  1 sttp1553 sttp1553     7392 Dec  9 10:44 linuxconf01.png
-rw-rw-r--  1 sttp1553 sttp1553     9736 Dec  9 10:44 linuxconf02.png
-rw-rw-r--  1 sttp1553 sttp1553   727366 Dec  9 10:48 linuxconf05.bmp
-rw-rw-r--  1 sttp1553 sttp1553    14743 Dec  9 10:46 linuxconf05.gif
-rw-rw-r--  1 sttp1553 sttp1553        0 Dec  9 10:48 linuxconf05.jpg
-rw-rw-r--  1 sttp1553 sttp1553    13024 Dec  9 10:46 linuxconf05.png
-rw-rw-r--  1 sttp1553 sttp1553  1477094 Dec  9 10:48 linuxconf05.ps
-rw-rw-r--  1 sttp1553 sttp1553   727366 Dec  9 10:49 linuxconf10.bmp
-rw-rw-r--  1 sttp1553 sttp1553    11870 Dec  9 10:49 linuxconf10.gif
-rw-rw-r--  1 sttp1553 sttp1553    10697 Dec  9 10:49 linuxconf10.png
-rw-rw-r--  1 sttp1553 sttp1553  1477094 Dec  9 10:49 linuxconf10.ps
-rw-rw-r--  1 sttp1553 sttp1553        0 Dec 18 13:26 lslaredhat70.txt
-rw-rw-r--  1 root root          2448 Dec  8 18:34 lspci.root
-rw-rw-r--  1 sttp1553 sttp1553     2435 Dec  8 18:34 lspci.v
-rw-rw-r--  1 sttp1553 sttp1553      715 Dec 18 13:25 lsredhat70.txt
drwx------  2 sttp1553 sttp1553     4096 Nov 26 12:00 nsmail
-rw-rw-r--  1 sttp1553 sttp1553  4784316 Nov 26 12:19 redhat701.ps
-rw-rw-r--  1 sttp1553 sttp1553  4784316 Nov 26 12:29 redhat704.ps
-rw-rw-r--  1 sttp1553 sttp1553  4784316 Nov 26 12:30 redhat705.ps
-rw-rw-r--  1 sttp1553 sttp1553     5264 Dec 18 09:22 redhat_bin.txt
-rw-rw-r--  1 sttp1553 sttp1553    10249 Dec 15 13:53 redhat_sbin.txt
-rw-rw-r--  1 sttp1553 sttp1553   107204 Dec 18 09:23 redhat_usr_bin.txt
-rw-rw-r--  1 sttp1553 sttp1553     9828 Dec 18 09:24 redhat_usr_sbin.txt
-rw-rw-r--  1 sttp1553 sttp1553  2359350 Nov 26 14:04 snapshot001.bmp
-rw-rw-r--  1 sttp1553 sttp1553   181309 Nov 26 14:04 snapshot001.gif
-rw-rw-r--  1 sttp1553 sttp1553    44122 Nov 26 14:04 snapshot001.png
-rw-rw-r--  1 sttp1553 sttp1553   504727 Nov 26 14:04 snapshot001.xbm
-rw-rw-r--  1 root root             0 Nov 22 18:42 z.z
```

Look at the start of this listing and you will see file names
that begin with a '.'

Command with multiple options

- ls -laR

This command will list all files, including hidden files, and do so recursively, i.e. it will do it for all subdirectories under the current directory. This generated over 700 lines of output on one system I tried it on. Sample output is not included.

Command with more than one option and one argument

- ls -laR /

As above, but start at the root directory. This generated over 97,000 lines of output on one SuSe system I ran it on. These are details on all of the files in the file system. Needless to say sample output is not included.

Getting help

This can be done in a number of ways. Both KDE and Gnome provide icons for on-line help. The other option is from a terminal session or console.

Graphical help

Under SuSe 6.4 Linux and the KDE the panel at the bottom contains the following two icons:

- book plus elephant
- book plus light bulb.

The first provides general Linux help. The second provides help on the K Desktop Environment.

Under SuSe Linux 7 the elephant and book have been replaced with a life belt.

Under Red Hat Linux and Gnome the panel contains an icon with a question mark. This brings up the Gnome help index.

All of the above provide structured information.

Terminal session or console

There are several ways of doing this:

- man command
- apropos string
- info command.

The first brings up the so-called manual pages. These are very good from the reference point of view but quite intimidating when all you want is a quick hint.

The second command searches the manual pages for commands that contain the string you've typed in. This can be very useful when you've forgotten the exact command or need a hint as to what command might be useful. This command is equivalent to

- man -k

The third provides a quite readable short description of the command and common options.

Basic DOS and Unix counterparts

The following table lists some of the common DOS commands and their Unix counterparts.

Action	DOS	Unix
show files	dir	ls
remove file	del	rm
remove directory	rmdir	rm -r
rename a file	rename	mv
	ren	
copy a file	copy	cp
contents of a file	type	cat
print a file	print	pr
edit a file	edit	see below
make a directory	md	mkdir
change directory	cd	cd
get help	help	man
	apropos	
date	date	date
time	time	date
display free disk space	chkdsk	df
find string in file	find	grep
	fgrep	
compare files	comp	diff
change file protection	attrib	chmod

It is assumed that you are familiar with most of the above. It is a good idea to bring up a terminal or console session and try some of the above out to see the similarities and differences between DOS and Unix.

Other Unix commands

The following are a few more example Unix commands.

Accessing the floppy drive

This can be done either from the desktop icon or the command prompt. The first thing to remember is that the Linux file system is different from a DOS file system and you have to mount a drive under a mount point. Typing

- df -k

will show you the file system and the following is the output from a SuSe 6.4 system.

```
Filesystem  1k-blocks  Used     Available  Use%  Mounted on
/dev/hda6   1320016    1026208  225672     82%   /
/dev/hda5   3745       1378     2167       39%   /boot
```

We will now look at making the floppy available.

From the desktop

Both Red Hat and SuSe provide desktop icons for accessing the floppy drive. Quite often just inserting a disk will mount the disk and bring up the file manager; this is very straightforward. Clicking on the floppy disk icon can also be used to mount the drive and bring up a file manager window. Both the KDE and Gnome screenshots in the last chapter show this.

From Unix as a Unix disk

We will look at this in a later chapter.

From Unix to a DOS floppy disk

The mtools package under SuSe Linux provides a simple set of DOS-like commands to enable you to read and write from a DOS-formatted floppy. Mtools is in the public domain and can be installed on other Linux distributions. Typing

- mdir a:

will provide access to the floppy without any preliminary mounting (assuming the default /etc/mtools.conf works on your machine). With mtools, you can change floppies too without unmounting and mounting.

Typing

- mdir a:

generates the following output:

```
Volume in drive A has no label
Volume Serial Number is 0A29-16CA
Directory for A:/
document      <DIR>       05-20-1991  16:56
reply         c00 64931   01-04-1995  15:45
resource frk  <DIR>       01-23-1995  13:59
              3 files     64 931 bytes
                          406 528 bytes free
```

The other commands are

- mattrib
- mbadblocks
- mcd
- mcopy
- mdel
- mdeltree
- mdir
- mdu
- mformat
- mkmanifest
- mlabel
- mmd
- mmount
- mmove
- mrd
- mread
- mren
- mtoolstest
- mtype.

Have a look at the man or info pages for more information.

Accessing the CD-Rom drive

This can be done either from a desktop icon or from the command prompt. The process is the same as for a floppy drive. Typing

- df -k

will show you the file system and the following is the output from a SuSe 6.4 system.

Filesystem	1k-blocks	Used	Available	Use%	Mounted on
/dev/hda6	1320016	1026208	225672	82%	/
/dev/hda5	3745	1378	2167	39%	/boot

We will look now at how to make the CD available in two ways.

From the desktop

Inserting a CD is often sufficient to mount the CD and bring up the file manager. Clicking on the CD icon on the desktop on the SuSe 6.4 system mounts the CD for you and brings up a file manager window. The KDE screenshot in the last chapter shows this. Typing

- df -k

now generates the following output on this system.

Filesystem	1k-blocks	Used	Available	Use%	Mounted on
/dev/hda6	1320016	1026212	225668	82%	/
/dev/hda5	3745	1378	2167	39%	/boot
/dev/hdc	635226	635226	0	100%	/cdrom

- Typing

ls -la /cdrom

will now show the files on the CD.

Both Red Hat and SuSe provide a desktop icon for the CD drive. This is obviously the easiest way of accessing the drive.

From raw Unix

We first need to mount the drive. The following command is an example taken from the SuSe 6.4 Linux system above:

- mount -t -iso9660 /dev/cdrom /cdrom
  - -t
  - -iso9660 type
  - /dev/cdrom - device
  - /cdrom - directory

Only root can do this by default. We will look into this in more detail in a later chapter.

The following command

- ls -la /cdrom

will now show the contents of the CD.

The following command will provide details of the mounted file systems:

- df -k

including the CD and this is the same as achieved above using the desktop icon to mount the CD.

The following command will unmount the CD:

- umount /cdrom

We will look in a later chapter at making the CD accessible to all users using the mount command.

The following is sample output from a Red Hat 7 system from typing

- df -k

after using the floppy and CD icons to access the drives. This is the system with a partitionless install.

Note that the mount point names are different from the SuSe system.

Filesystem	1k-blocks	Used	Available	Use%	Mounted on
/dev/loop1	2015824	1073528	839896	57%	/
/dev/fd0	1412	1119	221	84%	/mnt/floppy
/dev/hdc	246254	246254	0	100%	/mnt/cdrom

Text editors

There are a number of editors provided with a Linux system. It is convenient to categorize them as

- screen-based editors that run under the X-Windowing system where you can use the mouse to manipulate the file

- simple screen editors that run at the system prompt, and where actions are taken with the keyboard rather than the mouse
- command-driven editors that are complex and powerful.

The easiest to use are the screen editors that come with the KDE and Gnome windowing systems.

SuSe kedit

This is the default screen editor under SuSe Linux. It can be invoked in a variety of ways including:

- kedit from a console window when running the KDE
- clicking on a file with the appropriate file extension within the file manager

and the following is a screen shot that highlights the key features.

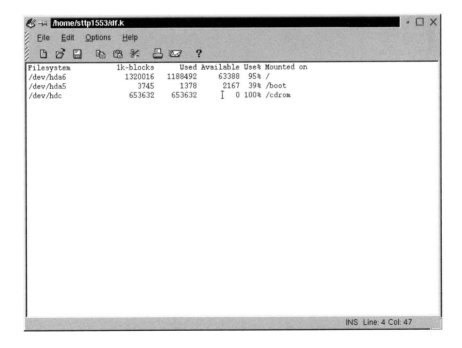

Red Hat gedit

This is an option under Red Hat Linux. It can be invoked by typing

- gedit

from a console window when running Gnome. This is shown below.

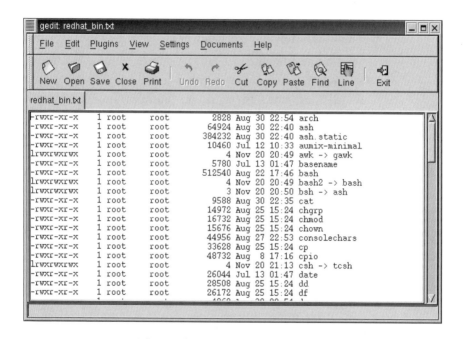

The default editor within the file manager is Emacs. We will look at this editor in a later chapter.

Pico

This is a simple editor on most Linux distributions. It can be run within a console window with or without a windows manager. The following screen shows its main features.

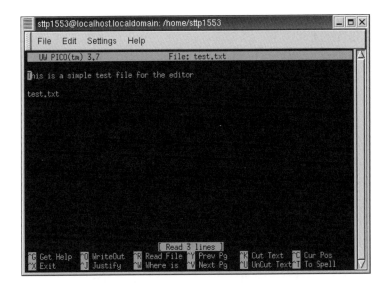

Pico is a simple screen text editor based on the Pine message system composer. Commands are displayed at the bottom of the screen and context-sensitive help is provided.

Editing commands are entered using control-key combinations. The editor has five basic features:

- paragraph justification
- searching
- block cut/paste
- spelling checker
- file browser.

Type pico at the system prompt and try it out.

vi

This is a powerful editor and can be found on most Linux systems. I've never found a Linux or Unix system without vi. We will come back to this editor in a later chapter.

Emacs

This is another powerful editor. It is seen by many as a better alternative to vi. Again, we will look at this editor in a later chapter.

GNU Emacs is a version of Emacs, written by the author of the original (PDP-10) Emacs, Richard Stallman. The primary documentation of GNU Emacs is in the GNU Emacs Manual, which you can read on-line using Info, a subsystem of Emacs.

Which one should I use?

It is worthwhile becoming familiar with both types of screen editor and one of vi or Emacs.

Bibliography

There are a lot of books about Linux and Unix. There is also a lot of information on the web. The best place to start is:

- http://www.linux.org

The documentation home page is

- http://www.linux.org/docs/index.html

The basic books home page is

- http://www.linux.org/books/basic.html

You may also find this site useful:

- http://unixhelp.ed.ac.uk/

Also have a look at:

- http://www.linux.org/docs/ldp/faq.html

Chapter 7

System Administration

The aim of this chapter is to look briefly at system administration.

This can be done in a number of ways:

- raw Unix
- system management tools
    ○ SuSe provide YaST
    ○ Red Hat provide Linuxconf.

We will look at each in turn after looking at the Filesystem Hierarchy Standard.

The Filesystem Hierarchy Standard (FHS)

It has probably become apparent by now that Linux and Unix systems are put together in a number of ways. They are sufficiently similar to give you encouragement and sufficiently different to be incredibly frustrating at times.

The FHS defines a common arrangement of the directories and files in Unix-like systems. It has been adopted by a number of developers, and its take-up is growing.

Their home address is:

- http://www.pathname.com/fhs

I would visit and have a look at the information they provide. If you have difficulties with the PDF version of the manual try:

- http://www.pathname.com/fhs/2.1/fhs-toc.html

Basic concepts

The following information is covered now to enable you to work your way around the Unix file system. Don't worry about assimilating it all at once. Refer to it as and when you need to.

The following four concepts are fundamental:

- shareable – shared by one or more users of the system
- unshareable – restricted to one system or user, e.g. file locks
- static – system components that don't change without explicit action, e.g. binaries, libraries, etc.
- variable – system components that change, e.g. system logs, user files.

The following table summarizes the above.

	shareable	unshareable
static	/usr	/etc
	/opt	/boot
variable	/var/mail	/var/run
	/var/spoll/news	/var/lock

The directory structure

The recommendation in the FHS manual is that the root directory file system should contain enough to be able to boot, restore, recover and repair the system when necessary.

/bin – essential system commands

System commands that are used by both the system administrator and general users.

/boot – static boot loader files

This directory contains all the files necessary for the boot process. The configuration files and map installer are excluded.

/dev – device files

All device and special files.

/etc – host-specific system configuration information

System-specific configuration files.

/home – user home directories

User home directories.

/lib – essential shared libraries and kernel modules

This should contain the shared library images required to boot the system and run the commands in the root file system.

/mnt – mount point

This is the directory to mount temporary file systems.

/opt – additional application packages

Third party software would be installed under this directory.

/root – home directory for super user

Home directory for the super user.

/sbin – essential system binaries

System binaries. Ordinary users should not have to put /sbin in their path.

/tmp – temporary files

Temporary files.

/usr – secondary hierarchy

This is the second major component of the file system.

/X11R6 – X-Windows system
X-Windows software.

/bin – user commands
Most user commands.

/games – games
Games.

/include – header files
Standard C header files.

/lib – libraries
Object files, libraries and internal binaries that are not intended to be executed directly by users.

/local – local hierarchy
System administrator use for installing local software.

/sbin – non-essential system binaries
Non-essential system binaries.

/share – hardware-specific data
Architecture-independent data.

/src – source code
Source code.

/var – variable data

The following is a directory listing from a Red Hat system.

```
arpwatch     cache        catman       db           gated
gdm          kerberos     lib          local        lock
log          mars_nwe     named        nis          preserve
run          spool        state        tmp          yp
```

SuSe file system

The following is taken from a SuSe Linux system.

```
drwxr-xr-x 19 root  root   4096 Feb 16  2000  .
drwxr-xr-x 19 root  root   4096 Feb 16  2000  ..
drwxr-xr-x  2 root  root   4096 Feb 16  2000  bin
drwxr-xr-x  3 root  root   1024 Feb 16  2000  boot
drwxr-xr-x  2 root  root   4096 Feb 16  2000  cdrom
drwxr-xr-x  6 root  root  32768 Apr  4  17:16 dev
drwxr-xr-x 29 root  root   4096 Sep 18  14:25 etc
drwxr-xr-x  2 root  root   4096 Feb 16  2000  floppy
drwxr-xr-x  3 root  root   4096 Feb 16  2000  home
drwxr-xr-x  6 root  root   4096 Feb 16  2000  lib
drwxr-xr-x  2 root  root  16384 Feb 16  2000  lost+found
drwxr-xr-x  2 root  root   4096 Feb 16  2000  mnt
drwxr-xr-x 12 root  root   4096 Feb 16  2000  opt
dr-xr-xr-x 64 root  root      0 Apr  4  17:15 proc
drwx—x—x    9 root  root   4096 Apr  2  12:33 root
drwxr-xr-x  5 root  root   4096 Feb 16  2000  sbin
drwxrwxrwt  4 root  root   4096 Sep 18  13:54 tmp
drwxr-xr-x 24 root  root   4096 Feb 16  2000  usr
drwxr-xr-x 18 root  root   4096 Feb 16  2000  var
```

Red Hat file system

The following is taken from a Red Hat Linux system.

```
rwxr-xr-x  20 root  root   4096 Aug 31 15:06 .
drwxr-xr-x 20 root  root   4096 Aug 31 15:06 ..
drwxr-xr-x  2 root  root   4096 Feb 17 2000  .automount
-rw-------  1 root  root     16 Aug 31 15:06 .bash_history
drwxr-xr-x  2 root  root   4096 Aug 30 20:04 bin
drwxr-xr-x  3 root  root   1024 Sep 11 17:36 boot
rwxr-xr-x   7 root  root  36864 Sep 11 17:37 dev
drwxr-xr-x 44 root  root   4096 Sep 13 17:04 etc
drwxr-xr-x  6 root  root   4096 Aug 30 20:04 home
drwxr-xr-x  4 root  root   4096 Aug 30 19:33 lib
drwxr-xr-x  2 root  root  16384 Aug 30 18:31 lost+found
drwxr-xr-x  2 root  root      0 Sep 11 17:36 misc
drwxr-xr-x  4 root  root   4096 Aug 30 18:36 mnt
drwxr-xr-x  2 root  root   4096 Aug 23 1999  opt
dr-xr-xr-x 56 root  root      0 Sep 11 17:36 proc
drwxr-x--- 11 root  root   4096 Sep 13 18:56 root
drwxr-xr-x  3 root  root   4096 Aug 30 20:04 sbin
drwxr-xr-x  3 root  root   4096 Aug 30 19:38 tftpboot
drwxrwxrwt  9 root  root   4096 Sep 18 04:02 tmp
drwxr-xr-x 22 root  root   4096 Aug 30 19:21 usr
drwxr-xr-x 22 root  root   4096 Aug 30 20:03 var
```

Secondary file system /usr – SuSe Linux

The following is taken from a SuSe Linux system.

```
drwxr-xr-x 24 root    root   4096 Feb 16 2000 .
drwxr-xr-x 19 root    root   4096 Feb 16 2000 ..
lrwxrwxrwx  1 root    root      5 Feb 16 2000 X11 ->> X11R6
drwxr-xr-x  8 root    root   4096 Feb 16 2000 X11R6
lrwxrwxrwx  1 root    root      5 Feb 16 2000 X386 ->> X11R6
drwxr-xr-x  2 root    root  12288 Feb 16 2000 bin
drwxr-xr-x  2 root    mail   4096 Feb 16 2000 cyrus
lrwxrwxrwx  1 root    root     10 Feb 16 2000 dict ->> share/dict
drwxr-xr-x  8 root    root   4096 Feb 16 2000 doc
drwxr-xr-x  2 empress root   4096 Feb 16 2000 empress
drwxr-xr-x  3 root    root   4096 Feb 16 2000 etc
```

```
drwxr-xr-x   4 root     root    4096 Feb 16 2000 games
drwxr-xr-x   5 root     root    4096 Feb 16 2000 i486-linux
drwxr-xr-x   5 root     root    4096 Feb 16 2000 i486-linux-libc5
drwxr-xr-x   5 root     root    4096 Feb 16 2000 i486-linux-libc6
drwxr-xr-x   5 root     root    4096 Feb 16 2000 i486-linuxaout
drwxr-xr-x   4 root     root    4096 Feb 16 2000 i486-suse-linux
drwxr-xr-x   5 root     root    4096 Feb 16 2000 i486-sysv4
drwxr-xr-x  30 root     root    4096 Feb 16 2000 include
drwxr-xr-x   2 root     root    4096 Feb 16 2000 info
drwxr-xr-x  48 root     root    8192 Feb 16 2000 lib
drwxr-xr-x   9 root     root    4096 Feb 16 2000 local
drwxr-xr-x  12 root     root    4096 Feb 16 2000 man
drwxr-xr-x   3 root     root    4096 Feb 16 2000 openwin
drwxr-xr-x   2 root     root    4096 Feb 16 2000 sbin
drwxr-xr-x  28 root     root    4096 Feb 16 2000 share
lrwxrwxrwx   1 root     root      12 Feb 16 2000 spool ->> ../var/spool
drwxr-xr-x   4 root     root    4096 Feb 16 2000 src
lrwxrwxrwx   1 root     root      10 Feb 16 2000 tmp ->> ../var/tmp
```

Secondary file system /usr – Red Hat Linux

The following is taken from a Red Hat Linux system.

```
drwxr-xr-x  22 root root  4096 Aug 30 19:21 .
drwxr-xr-x  20 root root  4096 Aug 31 15:06 ..
drwxr-xr-x   8 root root  4096 Mar  6 2000  X11R6
drwxr-xr-x   6 root root 36864 Aug 30 20:04 bin
drwxr-xr-x   2 root root  4096 Aug 30 19:21 boot
drwxr-xr-x   2 root root  4096 Aug 30 20:00 dict
drwxr-xr-x 353 root root  8192 Aug 31 14:35 doc
drwxr-xr-x   2 root root  4096 Feb  6 1996  etc
drwxr-xr-x   2 root root  4096 Aug 30 19:59 games
drwxr-xr-x   5 root root  4096 Aug 30 18:46 i386-glibc20-linux
drwxr-xr-x   4 root root  4096 Aug 30 18:50 i386-redhat-linux
drwxr-xr-x   3 root root  4096 Aug 30 19:21 i486-linux-libc5
drwxr-xr-x  85 root root  8192 Aug 30 20:04 include
drwxr-xr-x   2 root root 12288 Aug 30 20:04 info
drwxr-xr-x   7 root root  4096 Aug 30 19:20 kerberos
drwxr-xr-x  83 root root 24576 Aug 30 20:04 lib
drwxr-xr-x   7 root root  4096 Aug 30 19:44 libexec
drwxr-xr-x  11 root root  4096 Aug 30 18:36 local
drwxr-xr-x  14 root root  4096 Sep  1 04:02 man
drwxr-xr-x   2 root root  8192 Aug 30 20:04 sbin
```

```
drwxr-xr-x  90 root  root  4096  Aug 30 20:00  share
drwxr-xr-x   4 root  root  4096  Aug 30 19:20  src
lrwxrwxrwx   1 root  root    10  Aug 30 18:36  tmp ->> ../var/tmp
```

Refer to the above when looking for configuration files, log files and where to install software.

Accessing the floppy drive

This can be done in a variety of ways.

From the desktop

Both Red Hat and SuSe provide desktop icons for accessing the floppy drive, and drag and drop. This is very straight-forward. The KDE and GNOME screen shots showed this.

From Unix as a Unix disk

Remember that Unix file systems have to be mounted. We are thus looking at a two-stage process.

From Unix to a DOS floppy disk

The mtools package provides a simple set of DOS-like commands to enable you to read and write from a DOS-formatted floppy. This was covered in an earlier chapter. They are installed by default with SuSe Linux.

Putting a Unix file system on a floppy

This is done by typing

- /sbin/mke2fs /dev/fd0

You can now copy files to and from this floppy.

Accessing the CD-Rom drive

This can be done in a variety of ways.

From the desktop

Both Red Hat and SuSe provide a desktop icon for the CD drive, and drag and drop. This is obviously the easiest way of accessing the drive. Inserting a CD will bring up the desktop CD icon and start the file manager. This enables you to drag and drop files to and from the various parts of the file system.

From raw Unix

The first thing to do when working with files on a CD is to mount the drive. The following command is an example taken from a SuSe Linux system:

- mount -t -iso9660 /dev/cdrom /mnt/cdrom
- -t
- -iso9660
- /dev/cdrom
- /mnt/cdrom.

Only root can do this by default.

The following command

- ls -la /mnt/cdrom

will show the contents of the CD.

The following command will provide details of the mounted file systems:

- df -k

including the CD.

The following command will unmount the cd:

● umount /mnt/cdrom.

Making a boot floppy

It is recommended that you make boot floppies for the system. All magnetic media will fail. It is just a question of time.

Red Hat 7

The following are the steps required on the Red Hat partitionless system. Type

● uname -r

to obtain the details of the kernel. This returned the following information.

● 2.2.16-22

Then type

● mkbootdisk —device /dev/fd0 2.2.16-22

to actually create the boot floppy.

SuSe

This is best done under SuSe by using the YaST tool. Choose

    YaST

        System administration

            Kernel and boot configuration

                Create rescue disk

and have a blank floppy ready.

Linuxconf

Linuxconf is an administration system for the Linux operating system.

Home address is

- http://www.solucorp.qc.ca/linuxconf/

I recommend going there to get a real feel for what the product offers, and up to date information. Linuxconf is two things: a configuration utility (a user interface to do configuration tasks) and an activator. Here is a screenshot from a Red Hat system.

Linuxconf is involved at different points in the operation of your Linux workstation. Mostly, it has features to ensure that what you have configured is working.

This is the configuration option provided with the Red Hat systems I've used.

YaST – Yet another Setup Tool

SuSe provide YaST to make it easier to install and administer Linux. Help is normally available via F1 from most menus. English home page is:

- http://www.suse.de/en/

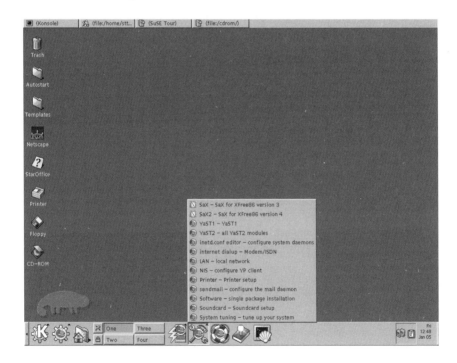

The following is what you see after YaST has started, in this case YaST 1 under SuSe 6.4

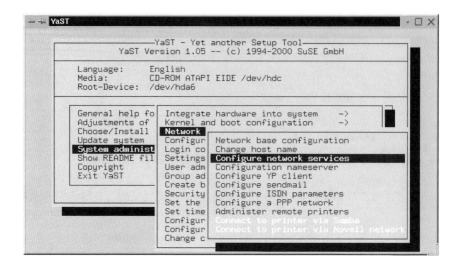

and by following the path YaST-> system admin-> network-> configure.

Note for Linuxconf and SuSe users

YaST does not collaborate well with other administration tools. To minimize problems you should edit the file /etc/rc.config and modify the line

ENABLE_SUSECONFIG=yes

to

ENABLE_SUSECONFIG=no

Otherwise YaST will overwrite many configuration changes you have done with Linuxconf.

Setting up a printer

This example involves setting up an HP Deskjet 690C. This is under both Red Hat 7 and SuSe 7. What is interesting is that during the original install of Linux, the printer was correctly identified by both installation programs. However neither installation completed the set-up to provide a working print service. We will look at each in turn.

Printer configuration under Red Hat

The following example is based on Red Hat Linux 7. Log in as root.

Choose

> Programs
>
>> System
>>
>>> Printer Tool

and the program detected the printer on

- /dev/lp0

and you will then have to choose the

- Input Filter

and you will have the chance to choose from a list. You also have to choose to set a number of other options including

- Resolution
- Paper Size

and a variety of printing options, depending on your printer.

You then need to start the lpd demon. This is a menu option from the Print Tool opening screen.

Typing

- lp filename

will then print the file. Have a look in

/var/spool/lpd/lp

to see what has been set up.

SuSe 7 live evaluation CD

The following example is taken from a SuSe 7 system. There are several ways to set up a printer including

1 – YaST

   Printer Setup

2 – YaST

   YaST 2

      Printer setup

3 – YaST

   YaST 1

      System administration

         Integrate hardware into system

         Printer

The key directory here is

- /var/spool/lpd

which is where the crucial files are installed. The following three commands for looking at printers are

- lp – print a file
- lpq – see what is in the print queue
- lprsetup – to delete printers.

Nothing printed after setting the printer up. What was interesting was that the correct files appeared to be in the

- /var/spool/lpd directory.

Using

- lpq

showed the file in the print queue. Typing

- lpq

later showed the print queue to be empty.

The next thing was to look for the log files. An

- ls -laR /var/spool/lpd | more

revealed one log file with non-zero length. This is that file:

```
Jan 21 13:42:10 suse lpd lp: ss_fork_and_or_exec: exec
'/var/lib/apsfilter/bin/y2prn_lp.upp—auto-lp' failed: No such
file or directory
```

```
Jan 21 13:42:10 suse lpd lp: Filter malfunctioned (exited with
status 2):
/var/lib/apsfilter/bin/y2prn_lp.upp—auto-lp -P'lp' -w80 -l66
-x0 -y0 -N'lpman.txt' -S'y2prn_lp.upp auto' -Y1 -D'Sun Jan 21
13:42:10 2001' -n'root' -h'suse.local' -J'lpman.txt ' -L'root'
-Ff -C'X' -q'1 ' -J'lpman.txt ' -C'X' -n'root' -h'suse.local'
-Ff '/var/spool/lpd/y2prn_lp.upp—auto-lp/acct'
```

The next thing was to try one of the other ways of setting up the printer. YaST 1 provided the most information. The file system where SuSe was trying to create files was read only. An examination showed that this was the CD.

Setting up a modem

We'll look at setting up two modems. These are

- PCI modem
- serial modem.

These are the cheapest available at this time. We will cover PCI modems in this chapter and serial modems in the next.

Some modem basics

The most common network protocol under Unix is TCP/IP.

When TCP/IP is used with a modem connection, Point to Point Protocol (PPP) is generally used.

If you have an ISDN connection then rawip and syncPPP are used. We will not be covering ISDN modems.

Most ISPs support PPP, and it is often the only supported protocol.

Both Red Hat and SuSe installed the necessary software to support networking via a modem. This includes:

- kernel support
- networking packages
- PPP packages
- wvdial.

The last thing that you need is obviously your user id and password for your ISP.

PCI modem

This is a Telepath Internet 56K WinModem. Neither Red Hat 7 nor SuSe 7 was able to automatically set up the PCI modem. SuSe have a section in the SuSe Handbook that covers how to do this. After trying this out I couldn't get it to work and eventually went to the wvdial website and had a look at their FAQ. At the time of writing these PCI modems weren't supported under Linux. The following is a paragraph from the wvdial FAQ.

- "If it's a PCI modem you're probably in for a wild ride trying to get it to work. There is provisional support for these in the newer kernels so you might strike lucky if you happen to have a supported model. Try PCIutils to help you get started."

I spent a while trying out the PCIutils program and decided to go no further. If you want a wild ride I recommend Space Mountain at Disneyland California.

The wvdial home page is

http://www.worldvisions.ca/wvdial/

The PCI utilities

The PCI utilities package contains a library for portable access to PCI bus configuration space and several utilities based on this library. The utilities include

- lspci
  - which displays detailed information about all PCI buses and devices in the system
- setpci
  - which allows you to read from and write to PCI device configuration registers.

The following shows the output of running

- lspci -v

as root on that system.

```
Gateway PII 350
00:00.0 Host bridge: Intel Corporation 440BX/ZX - 82443BX/ZX
Host bridge (rev 02)
   Subsystem: Intel Corporation 440BX/ZX - 82443BX/ZX Host
   bridge
   Flags: bus master, medium devsel, latency 64
   Memory at f8000000 (32-bit, prefetchable)
   Capabilities: [a0] AGP version 1.0

00:01.0 PCI bridge: Intel Corporation 440BX/ZX - 82443BX/ZX
AGP bridge (rev 02) (prog-if 00 [Normal decode])
   Flags: bus master, 66Mhz, medium devsel, latency 64
   Bus: primary=00, secondary=01, subordinate=01,
   sec-latency=64
   I/O behind bridge: 0000d000-0000dfff
   Memory behind bridge: fc200000-feafffff
   Prefetchable memory behind bridge: f2000000-f40fffff

00:07.0 ISA bridge: Intel Corporation 82371AB PIIX4 ISA (rev 02)
   Flags: bus master, medium devsel, latency 0

00:07.1 IDE interface: Intel Corporation 82371AB PIIX4 IDE
(rev 01) (prog-if 80 [Master])
   Flags: bus master, medium devsel, latency 64
   I/O ports at ffa0
```

```
00:07.2 USB Controller: Intel Corporation 82371AB PIIX4 USB
(rev 01) (prog-if 00 [UHCI])
    Flags: bus master, medium devsel, latency 0, IRQ 10
    I/O ports at ef80

00:07.3 Bridge: Intel Corporation 82371AB PIIX4 ACPI (rev 02)
    Flags: medium devsel

00:0c.0 Multimedia audio controller: Ensoniq ES1371
[AudioPCI-97] (rev 04)
    Subsystem: Gateway 2000: Unknown device 8030
    Flags: bus master, slow devsel, latency 64, IRQ 9
    I/O ports at ef00
    Capabilities: [dc] Power Management version 1

00:0e.0 Ethernet controller: 3Com Corporation 3c905B
100BaseTX [Cyclone] (rev 24)
    Subsystem: 3Com Corporation 3C905B Fast Etherlink XL
    10/100
    Flags: bus master, medium devsel, latency 32, IRQ 9
    I/O ports at ec00
    [virtual] Memory at febffc00 (32-bit, non-prefetchable)
    [disabled]
    Expansion ROM at febc0000 [disabled]
    Capabilities: [dc] Power Management version 1

00:10.0 Communication controller: Lucent Microelectronics
WinModem 56k (rev 01)
    Subsystem: GVC Corporation LT WinModem 56k Data+Fax
    Flags: bus master, medium devsel, latency 0, IRQ 10
    Memory at febff800 (32-bit, non-prefetchable)
    I/O ports at eff0
    I/O ports at e800
    Capabilities: [f8] Power Management version 2

01:00.0 VGA compatible controller: NVidia / SGS Thomson
(Joint Venture) Riva128 (rev 22) (prog-if 00 [VGA])
    Subsystem: Gateway 2000 STB Velocity 128
    Flags: bus master, 66Mhz, medium devsel, latency 64, IRQ 11
    Memory at fd000000 (32-bit, non-prefetchable)
    Memory at f3000000 (32-bit, prefetchable)
    Expansion ROM at fe400000 [disabled]
    Capabilities: [44] AGP version 1.0
```

and as can be seen they do quite a good job of providing information about the various PCI devices in the PC.

Setting up a sound card

The set-up of sound cards on a number of systems was attempted.

Avance Logic PCI Sound Card

This was with the ALS400 Audio chipset. No suitable driver could be found. Searching the sound driver database showed that the most recent was the ALS120. This did not work.

Creative Sound Blaster Audio PCI 64V

This card was picked up at install time and set up correctly with both the SuSE 7 evaluation CD install and the Red Hat 7 partitionless install.

Setting up a scanner

This was a USB port scanner. This was not supported at this time. See the next entry for a Web address for up to date information.

Setting up a Web camera

This was a USB port camera. This was not supported at this time.

See:

- http://www.linux-usb.org

for more information.

CD rewriter

This is an HP 9100 series CD rewriter. This was detected by the SuSe 7 evaluation CD install. I was unable to determine if there was any software capable of making use of the device as a CD rewriter. Software for SCSII devices exists, but I couldn't find any IDE-based software.

System start-up and shutdown

The system will need to be shutdown and restarted periodically. You will need to do this if you install new hardware or reconfigure the system. You should never press the reset button or turn the machine off. The major damage will be to the file system.

This is done using the shutdown command. This command can only be done as root. The two most common commands are

- shutdown -h now

and

- shutdown -r now

if you are the only user. The first actually halts the system and allows you to then power the system off. The second is used when you want to reboot the system.

If other users may be logged on then the following form is recommended

- shutdown -r +5 ' Please log off – System maintenance taking place'

the key additional parameters are +5 which is the number of minutes to shutdown and a text message that will appear to any users logged on. Now is equivalent to +0.

There are several run modes.

Run Level	Description
0	Shut the system down
1	Single user mode
2	Multi-user mode, no NFS
3	Full multi-user mode
5	Full multi-user mode with GUI
6	Reboot

Level 1 is used for resolving system problems. It is a very minimal system. If you want exact information about what comes up with each run level have a look in

- /etc/rc.d

and you will see a series of directories from rc0.d through rc6.d. There will be one or more files in each directory, depending on which version of Linux you have. Have a look at each file to get the exact set-up for your system.

Altering the default run level

You may want to alter the default run level at system start-up. Look at the

- /etc/inittab

file. Look for the

- initdefault

entry.

Making more memory available

Both the Red Hat 7 and SuSe 7 evaluation CD only made 64Mb of memory available to Linux on the Pentium II 350 with 192Mb of memory.

Typing

- linux mem=192M

at system boot up made all of the memory available.

On the Red Hat system this could be made permanent by editing the

- lilo.conf

in the

- /etc

directory on the boot floppy by adding

- append = "192M"

This can't be done on the CD for SuSe Linux.

Accessing a Windows partition

If you have gone for the dual boot option you may be interested in accessing the Windows side of the machine.

The SuSe 7 evaluation CD system provided desktop icons for the drives so access is very straightforward with this install. Here is the fstab file for that system:

```
/dev/ram2                     /            ext2     defaults                    1 1
none                          /proc        proc     defaults                    0 0
/dev/hdc                      /S.u.S.E.    iso9660  ro                          0 0
/dev/hda1                     /windows/C   vfat     noauto,user                 0 0
/dev/hda5                     /windows/D   vfat     noauto,user                 0 0
/dev/hdb1                     /windows/E   vfat     noauto,user                 0 0
devpts                        /dev/pts     devpts   defaults                    0 0
/dev/cdrom                    /cdrom       auto     ro,noauto,user,exec         0 0
/dev/cdrom1                   /cdrom1      auto     ro,noauto,user,exec         0 0
/dev/fd0                      /floppy      auto     noauto,user                 0 0
/windows/C/suselive.swp  swap             swap     defaults                    0 0
/windows/C/suselive.usr  /home            ext2     defaults,loop=/dev/loop1 0 0
```

This file is in

- /etc

Red Hat 7 provides two ways of doing this. Assuming that

- /dev/hda5

is the drive you are interested in and is drive E then typing

- mkdir /mnt/e

creates a mount point and

- mount -t vfat /dev/hda5 /mnt/e

will actually mount the drive for you. Access is restricted to root.

You can also use Linuxconf to provide more general access. Log in as root and before you start Linuxconf make a backup of the /etc/fstab file. Now start Linuxconf. Here is the opening screen shot.

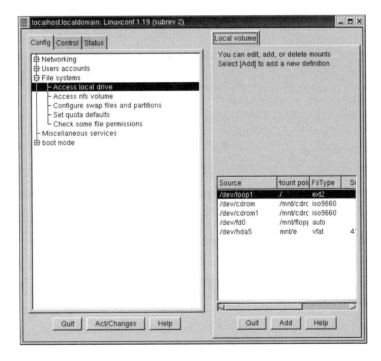

Click on Add at the bottom right and you will see the following screen.

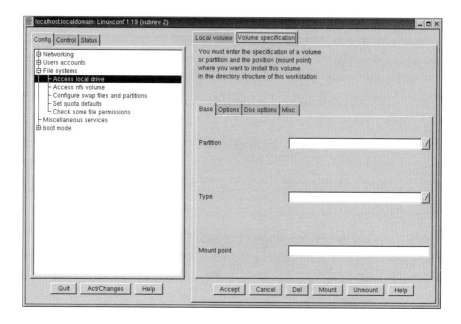

Work through each tab and fill in all of the necessary details. Here is the fstab file from that system after running Linuxconf.

```
# LOOP1: /dev/hdb1 vfat /redhat.img
/dev/loop1        /                  ext2    defaults        1 1
/dev/cdrom        /mnt/cdrom         iso9660 noauto,owner,ro 0 0
/dev/cdrom1       /mnt/cdrom1        iso9660 noauto,owner,ro 0 0
/dev/fd0          /mnt/floppy        auto    noauto,owner    0 0
none              /proc              proc    defaults        0 0
none              /dev/pts           devpts  gid=5,mode=620  0 0
/initrd/loopfs /rh-swap.img swap     swap    defaults        0 0
/dev/hda5         mnt/e              vfat
    exec,dev,suid,ro,conv=auto,uid=500,gid=500               1 1
```

Miscellaneous

There were a number of odd problems that occurred whilst setting up the various systems.

On one system the installation of some additional software (about 300Mb) used up all of the user file space. Things ran at the time of the install. A subsequent reboot meant that the system did not come up properly and some of the services were not started. When the console window came up, typing

- startx

didn't do anything.

A

- df -k

showed that there was no file space left. Removing some of the additionally installed software freed up 150Mb and this sorted the problem out. This was one of the systems with a 2Gb hard disk.

On the same system I tried setting up an old US Robotics modem that I had been given. Most of the set up described for the Miracom modem worked. It was only at the last stage when using wvdial that things wouldn't work. It turned out that the modem was faulty.

Bibliography

The obvious place to start are the manuals that came with your distribution. The next places to look are the manuals and help files that came with the distribution. Chapter 4 contains details of these.

Finally there are books and Web sources. Two books you might like to consider are:

- Welsh, M. and Kaufman,L., *Running Linux*, O'Reilly.
- LeBlanc, D., *Linux System Administration*, Black Book, CoriolisOPen Press.

The web place to start is:

- http://www.linux.org

Happy reading!

Chapter

8

Networking and Security

The aim of this chapter is to look at networking and security.

This chapter looks briefly at setting up, managing and diagnosing problems with a network. Dial-up networking is covered in an earlier chapter.

Networking basics

There are some concepts that we need to look at to enable us to set up networking. As one of the cheapest and most widely used ways of networking is done using Ethernet technology we will cover this in sufficient depth to enable us to connect to a network at work or set up a local network at home.

Ethernet card MAC address.

Each Ethernet card has a unique address. This is called a MAC address. The following is a MAC address taken from a 3COM 3c509 card.

- 00:A0:24:47:F3:CD

In a work environment it is common to bind MAC addresses to IP addresses. This enables the network people to determine who is doing what. This is often done using Dynamic Host Configuration Protocol (DHCP). This is looked at in more depth later.

IP address and other network information

As we mentioned in an earlier chapter there are several classes of networks:

- Class A – range 1.0.0.0 through 127.0.0.0
  - approximately 1.6 million hosts.

- Class B – range 128.0.0.0 through 191.255.0.0
  - ○ 16065 networks with 65534 hosts.
- Class C – range 192.0.0.0 through 223.255.255.0
  - ○ approximately 2 million networks with up to 254 hosts.
- Numbers in the range 224 through 239
  - ○ multicast.
  - ○ Over 239 are reserved.

You can assign the following if you are using a local network.

- Class A – 10.0.0.0 through 10.255.255.255
- Class B – 172.16.0.0 through 172.31.255.255
- Class C – 192.168.0.0 through 192.168.255.255

You can't use some IP addresses because they are used by the network.

Basic network terminology

The following provides a simple description of some of the common networking terms.

IP address

Each device on the network must have an IP address to be able to communicate with the others.

DHCP

This stands for Dynamic Host Configuration Protocol. One of its uses is for automatic allocation of IP addresses. At King's it is used in the newer parts of the College to provide this. Other older parts of the network require manual or hard-wired IP addresses. This is not as flexible and means that if someone moves from one part of the building to another then they will probably require human intervention to get them network-connected again.

Host name

Each machine is generally given a name that is meaningful.
It is much easier to work with mnemonics than IP addresses.

Subnets

Management of a network would be much more difficult
without using subnets. They provide a mechanism for
decentralizing network management.

Subnet masks

For communication to work each system on a subnet needs
the same mask.

Default gateway

If the system is to communicate with systems that are not on
the same subnet a gateway is normally provided.

Broadcast address

To avoid broadcast problems the broadcast address of every
computer on a network must be the same.

Domain Name Server (DNS)

It is common to provide links between IP addresses and
systems via meaningful names. This is normally done using
a domain name server.

Networking at home

Here we will look at setting up two or more systems at home. The assumption is that you have Ethernet cards and a hub. This is a relatively low-cost and very useful way to set up your machines. The information is based on setting up the following systems

- P75, 32Mb memory, Ethernet card, single booting SuSe Linux 6.4
- Cyrix, 48Mb memory, Ethernet card, dual booting SuSe Linux 7.0
- Intel Pentium PII 350, Ethernet card, triple booting Windows 98, SuSe Linux 7.0 Evaluation system, running from CD, Red Hat Linux 7 booting from floppy.

As these are on a local network the set up is very straightforward.

Preliminaries

You need to decide on the following:

- IP address for each machine
- as they are all on the same subnet choose a subnet mask
- give the machines a name.

We will look at each in turn.

IP address

Two of the machines already had IP addresses under Windows. I stuck with the same addresses.

- Cyrix – 10.0.0.1
- PII 350 – 10.0.0.2
- P75 – 10.0.0.4

I don't know why I missed out 10.0.0.3!

Subnet mask

As the two Windows machines were already networked I stuck with the existing subnet mask – 255.255.255.0

Names

Give each machine a name.

Network administration via graphical interfaces

Both SuSe and Red Hat provide ways of doing network administration from the system administration menu systems.

SuSe 6.4

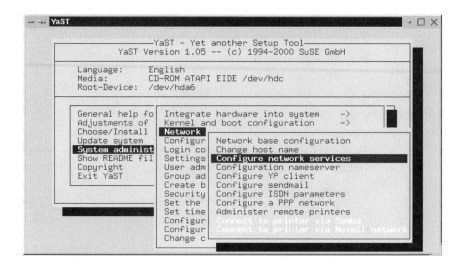

SuSe 7

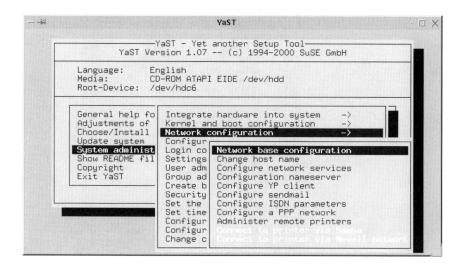

As can be seen they are very similar.

Ensure that you log in as root under Red Hat. Some of the system administration tools do not appear if you are logged in as a normal user.

You can access them by doing a su from a console window and actually typing the command, e.g.

linuxconf

would bring up the Linux configuration tool.

Red Hat 7

The following screen shot is from running Linuxconf on a Red Hat 7 system

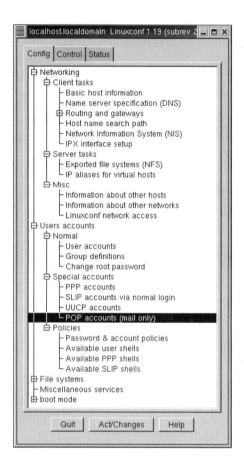

Dial-up networking at home

There are three systems at home and each has a different type of modem. We will look at each in turn.

SuSe 6.4 – external Miricom modem

This was straightforward to set up using YaST and wvdial. Start YaST and follow the links:

System administration

Integrate hardware into system

Modem configuration

You need to know which serial port the modem is connected to – in this case com1. With an external modem make sure that the modem is plugged in, switched on and you have connected the modem to the phone line. This will start SuSeconfig and you will see a set of scripts running.

Next choose

> System administration

>> Network configuration

>> Configure PPP network

This will bring up the following screen:

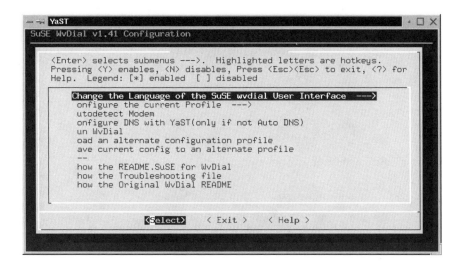

The key ones are

> Configure the current Profile

> Autodetect Modem

> Save current config ...

amongst others. You need to

> Configure the current Profile and this will require setting

>> Phone number

Area code

Account name

Password

Automatic DNS – Yes

Dial method – Tone Dial

Modem on PBX – No

PAP/CHAP authentication mode – the most common.

The following screenshot shows some details of the above.

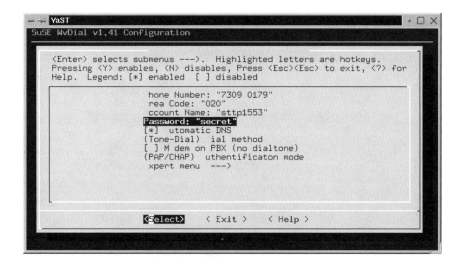

Autodetect modem will then look for the modem and deter-mine a number of settings including maximum line speed.

Running wvdial then starts the connection and Netscape was started to verify that things were working.

You should then save the current configuration. The maximum line speed chosen was 38400.

You should now start YaST and choose

System administration

User Administration

and type in the name of each user that you want to have modem access. The following is a screenshot of this.

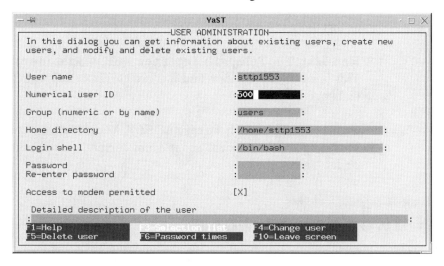

These users will then be able to run wvdial from a console window.

SuSe 7 – internal 14400 bps Data Fax modem

This was straightforward to set up using YaST and wvdial. The set up was similar to the previous. Choose the YaST 1 set up rather than YaST 2; it seems more straightforward. The following screenshot is taken from this system.

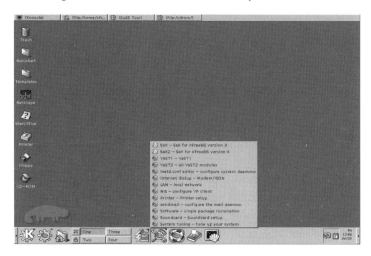

Do not choose

- Internet Dialup – Modem/ISDN

as this did not work reliably.

Red Hat 7 – Telepath Internet 56K WinModem
This is a PCI Win Modem and it is not currently supported by Linux.

SuSE 7 – Telepath Internet 56K WinModem
This is a PCI Win Modem and it is not currently supported under Linux

Networking at work

You will need to contact your local network administrator. Each organization will have its own rules and recommendations for network access.

Network set-up programs

Both SuSe and Red Hat provide network set-up programs. These should be used as they automate much of the process for you. You have seen screenshots of using YaST and Linuxconf.

Networking utilities

There are a number of networking utilities including:

- ifconfig

and

- netstat.

Try running these commands to see what information is provided.

These would only normally be used when sorting out networking problems. See the man pages for more information.

Security

The security of your system is important. This chapter looks at a couple of ways of removing some of the more obvious ways of compromising your system.

The PC itself is not very secure. They are small and can be stolen quite easily. So the first aspect of security is the actual machine itself. There is also the issue of media failing. Nothing lasts forever. One work machine was stolen which had the data from a European study into kidney damage. There were 3500 files totalling 280Mb. The system was replaced and the data copied over from a backup and the overall system was live again within a week. So backup of files is important. We will look into this in a subsequent chapter.

The next thing to consider is how easy it is to compromise the actual system. Most people do not bother with BIOS passwords or altering the actual boot settings on the machine so that it can't boot from a floppy or CD.

If the machine is accessible there is also the problem of powering the system off or hitting the reset button.

In a work environment there is the issue of malicious damage and of people using systems to attack people elsewhere, e.g. to launch a denial of service attack.

A major part of security is therefore the effort you are prepared to put in.

No network connection

The most secure set-up is no network connection. If you don't want to spend additional time and effort on system management then this is a good option. To see some of the problems with Linux visit the SuSe and Red Hat sites and look at the patches that are available.

The following is the SuSe home site (English)

- http://www.suse.com/en/

Follow the links to

- http://www.suse.com/en/support/download/updates/index.html

They have a security page too:

- http://www.suse.com/en/support/security/index.html

The following is a selection of Red Hat addresses that you should look at:

- http://www.redhat.com/support/errata/
- http://www.redhat.com/support/errata/rh7-errata-security.html
- http://www.redhat.com/support/errata/rh7-errata-bugfixes.html

The question that you have to ask is do you have the time to keep the system secure?

Firewalls

You may be lucky and have a firewall installed at work. This makes it much more difficult for external people to hack into your systems. If that is the case then you might not need to do very much on the systems side. Ask your local network team about this.

Network connection

If you are going to have a network connection then there are a number of things that you can do that will reduce the probability of hacking.

TCP wrappers

TCP wrappers require the set up of the following three files:

- inetd.conf
- hosts.deny
- hosts.allow.

The inetd.conf contains details of what services you want to make available and the programs that are used to provide these services.

The basic idea is that the hosts.deny files contains details of who you don't want to have access to your system. The hosts.allow file contains details of those people who you do want to have access.

However nothing is perfect because IP spoofing is possible.

inetd.conf

This file controls what services are running on your machine. A couple of sample listings are shown below.

```
#
# inetd.conf  This file describes the services that will be
# available
# through the INETD TCP/IP super server. To re-configure
# the running INETD process, edit this file, then send the
# INETD process a SIGHUP signal.
#
# Version: @(#)/etc/inetd.conf          3.10     05/27/93
#
# Authors: Original taken from BSD UNIX 4.3/TAHOE.
# Fred N. van Kempen, <<waltje@uwalt.nl.mugnet.org>>
#
# Modified for Debian Linux by Ian A. Murdock
# <<imurdock@shell.portal.com>>
#
# Modified for RHS Linux by Marc Ewing <<marc@redhat.com>>
#
# <<service_name>> <<sock_type>> <<proto>> <<flags>> <<user>>
```

```
<<server_path>>
<<args>>
#
# Echo, discard, daytime, and chargen are used primarily for
# testing.
#
# To re-read this file after changes, just do a 'killall -
# HUP inetd'
#
#echo       stream   tcp   nowait   root   internal
#echo       dgram    udp   wait     root   internal
#discard    stream   tcp   nowait   root   internal
#discard    dgram    udp   wait     root   internal
#daytime    stream   tcp   nowait   root   internal
#daytime    dgram    udp   wait     root   internal
#chargen    stream   tcp   nowait   root   internal
#chargen    dgram    udp   wait     root   internal
#time       stream   tcp   nowait   root   internal
#time       dgram    udp   wait     root   internal
#
# These are standard services.
#
ftp        stream tcp nowait root /usr/sbin/tcpd in.ftpd -l -a
telnet     stream tcp nowait root /usr/sbin/tcpd in.telnetd
#
# Shell, login, exec, comsat and talk are BSD protocols.
#
#shell     stream tcp nowait root /usr/sbin/tcpd in.rshd
#login     stream tcp nowait root /usr/sbin/tcpd in.rlogind
#exec      stream tcp nowait root /usr/sbin/tcpd in.rexecd
#comsat    dgram  udp wait   root /usr/sbin/tcpd in.comsat
#talk      dgram  udp wait nobody tty /usr/sbin/tcpd in.talkd
#ntalk     dgram  udp wait nobody.tty /usr/sbin/tcpd in.ntalkd
#dtalk     stream tcp wait nobody.tty /usr/sbin/tcpd in.dtalkd
#
# Pop and imap mail services et al
#
#pop-2     stream tcp nowait root /usr/sbin/tcpd ipop2d
#pop-3     stream tcp nowait root /usr/sbin/tcpd ipop3d
#imap      stream tcp nowait root /usr/sbin/tcpd imapd
#
# The Internet UUCP service.
#
#uucp stream tcp nowait uucp /usr/sbin/tcpd /usr/lib/uucp/uucico -l
#
# Tftp service is provided primarily for booting.  Most sites
```

```
# run this only on machines acting as "boot servers." Do not
# uncomment
# this unless you *need* it.
#
#tftp      dgram  udp wait root   /usr/sbin/tcpd in.tftpd
#bootps    dgram  udp wait root   /usr/sbin/tcpd bootpd
#
# Finger, systat and netstat give out user information which
# may be
# valuable to potential "system crackers". Many sites choose
# to disable
# some or all of these services to improve security.
#
#finger  stream tcp  nowait  nobody /usr/sbin/tcpd in.fingerd
#cfinger stream tcp  nowait  root   /usr/sbin/tcpd in.cfingerd
#systat  stream tcp  nowait  guest  /usr/sbin/tcpd /bin/ps -auwwx
#netstat stream tcp  nowait guest /usr/sbin/tcpd /bin/netstat -f inet
#
# Authentication
#
# identd is run standalone now
#
#auth stream tcp wait  root /usr/sbin/in.identd in.identd -e -o
#
# End of inetd.conf
# linuxconf stream tcp wait root /bin/linuxconf linuxconf —http
#swat     stream  tcp  nowait.400    root /usr/sbin/swat swat
```

A careful look at this file shows that the only two services provided are ftp and telnet.

hosts.deny

Here is an example of a hosts.deny file.

```
# See tcpd(8) and hosts_access(5) for a description.
# ypserv: ALL
http-rman : ALL EXCEPT LOCAL
ALL: ALL
```

This denies all access from the outside world.

hosts.allow

Here is an example of a hosts.allow file. You just add the addresses you will accept access from and the type of service they have access to.

```
# See tcpd(8) and hosts_access(5) for a description.
# ypserv: 127.0.0.0/255.0.0.0 10.0.0.0/255.0.0.0
# (ALL EXCEPT in.fingerd) EXCEPT in.identd : ALL :
# (safe_finger -l @%h 2>>&1| \
#                /bin/mail -s "%d-%h %u" root) &
ALL: 199.99.99.1
ALL: 199.99.99.2
ALL: 199.99.99.3
```

Note that the IP addresses are made up.

Sendmail

Both Red Hat and SuSe will install a working sendmail. Sendmail is one of the most vulnerable parts of your system. We will look at what can be done to minimize problems in this area.

The first thing to do is see if sendmail is actually running.

- ps -ef | grep sendmail

will show this; ps gives a snapshot of the current processes. The ef options provide more detailed information. The output is then piped into grep and we look for the string 'sendmail'.

Here is an example taken from a SuSe 6.4 system:

```
root      175  1    0  15:17 ?      00:00:00 sendmail:
                                    accepting connections on port 25
sttp1553  669  612  0  15:57 pts/0 00:00:00 grep sendmail
```

The next place to look is:

/etc/rc.d/init.d

SuSe Linux 6.4 arranges init.d to be a link and the sendmail script is in the /etc/rc.d directory.

Red Hat 7 Linux has a genuine init.d subdirectory and the sendmail script is in that directory.

In both cases rename the script to stop it running, e.g.

- mv sendmail disabled_sendmail

will do the trick.

Note that local mail is still available, i.e. you can use one of the mail clients to other users of the system.

Other security options

Secure Shell

The Secure Shell Community Site is

- http://www.ssh.org/

This replaces

- rsh
- rlogin
- rcp
- telnet
- rexec
- rcp
- ftp.

It encrypts all traffic and provides a variety of levels of authentication. Some of the main features include

- secure remote logins
- file copying
- tunneling TCP and X11 traffic.

You will also need to install secure clients on each machine that needs access to your Linux system. This obviously involves a fair bit of work.

Kerberos

One of the main things hackers need are passwords. Those that are sent without encryption can be easily read and used. Kerberos provides encryption that stops your password from being sent over the network in the clear. Kerberos is a network authentication protocol. It is designed to provide strong authentication for client/server applications by using secret-key cryptography. A free implementation of this protocol is available from the Massachusetts Institute of Technology. Kerberos is available in many commercial products as well. Visit

- http://web.mit.edu/kerberos/www/

for more information.

Shadow password

Most recent Linux systems will use a shadow file. The two files of interest here are

- /etc/passwd
- /etc/shadow.

The following output from running ls -la taken from two systems.

SuSe 6.4

```
-rw-r—r—  1 root     root      2547 Dec  8 15:28 /etc/passwd
-rw-r——-  1 root     shadow    1216 Dec  8 15:28 /etc/shadow
```

Red Hat 7

```
-rw-r—r—  1 root     root       795 Nov 20 21:18 /etc/passwd
-rw——-—-  1 root     root       661 Nov 20 21:18 /etc/shadow
```

Try

- cat /etc/passwd
- cat /etc/shadow

to see what happens.

System logs

The system logs are important for troubleshooting and to see if your system has been hacked. There are two issues here: what is logged and the actual log files.

syslog.conf

The following is an example of a syslog.conf file from a Red Hat 6.2 installation.

```
# Log all kernel messages to the console.
# Logging much else clutters up the screen.

# kern.*     /dev/console

# Log anything (except mail) of level info or higher.
# Don't log private authentication messages!
*.info;mail.none;news.none;authpriv.none/var/log/messages

# The authpriv file has restricted access.

authpriv.*          /var/log/secure

# Log all the mail messages in one place.

mail.*              /var/log/maillog
# Everybody gets emergency messages, plus log them on another
# machine.
*.emerg              *

# Save mail and news errors of level err and higher in a
# special file.
uucp,news.crit                  /var/log/spooler
```

```
# Save boot messages also to boot.log
local7.*                        /var/log/boot.log

#
# INN
#
news.=crit                      /var/log/news/news.crit
news.=err                       /var/log/news/news.err
news.notice                     /var/log/news/news.notice
```

Have a look at the syslog.conf file for your system to see what
is being logged and where the actual files are.

/var/log

The first place to look is in

- /var/log

Here is the output from running

- ls -la

on a SuSe 6 Linux system.

```
total 864
drwxr-xr-x 4 root    root    4096 Jan 11 16:37 .
drwxr-xr-x 18 root   root    4096 Jul 30 15:12 ..
-rw-r—r—   1 root    root    1487 Jul 30 15:44 Config.bootup
-rw-r—r—   1 root    root    3323 Jan 11 09:41 boot.msg
-rw-------  1 root    root   12048 Jan 11 18:52 faillog
drwxr-xr-x 2 root    root    4096 Jul 30 15:41 httpd
-rw-r—r—   1 root    root       0 Jul 30 14:44 httpd.access_log
-rw-r—r—   1 root    root       0 Jul 30 14:44 httpd.error_log
-rw-rw-r—  1 root    tty   146584 Jan 11 18:52 lastlog
-rw-r-----  1 root    root   82869          Jan 11 09:41 mail
-rw-r-----  1 root    root  273816 Jan 11 18:52 messages
drwxr-xr-x 2 news    news    4096 Jul 30 14:31 news
-rw-r—r--  1 root    root     616 Nov 26 13:05 sendmail.st
-rw-------  1 wwwrun  root       0 Jul 30 14:44 ssl_scache.dir
-rw-------  1 wwwrun  root       0 Jul 30 14:44 ssl_scache.pag
-rw-r-----  1 root    root  103758 Jan 11 09:41 warn
-rw-rw-r—  1 root    tty   332544 Jan 11 18:52 wtmp
-rw-rw-r—  1 root    tty    11959 Nov 26 13:00 wtmp-20001126.gz
```

```
-rw-r—-   1 root    root       0 Mar 24   2000 xdm.errors
-rw-r-r—   1 root    root     315 Sep 20 13:24 y2log
```

Have a look at

- messages

in an editor. Note the file permissions on these files.

Also have a look at:

- warn

Here is a section of that file:

```
Nov 28 16:45:36 suse sendmail[176]: NOQUEUE: low on space
(have 0, SMTP-DAEMON needs 101 in /var/spool/mqueue)
Nov 28 16:46:06 suse last message repeated 2 times
Nov 28 16:47:06 suse last message repeated 4 times
Nov 28 16:48:06 suse last message repeated 4 times
Nov 28 16:49:06 suse last message repeated 4 times
Nov 28 16:50:06 suse last message repeated 4 times
Nov 28 16:51:06 suse last message repeated 4 times
Nov 28 16:52:06 suse last message repeated 4 times
```

This was when I was running out of space due to the installation of software that filled up the disk.

Have a look at these files fairly quickly after the install. You need to see what the files look like before your system is compromised.

Summary

SuSe provide YaST to help with network set up and Red Hat provide Linuxconf.

Security takes time. You need to consider how much time you want to spend on keeping a system secure. I use computer systems as a tool. Here is an extract from an email received at King's.

```
Identities concealed to protect the hapless...
    Date: Mon, 13 Nov 2000 10:22:31 -0000 From: "Sxxx, Axxx
J" <<Axxx.J.Sxxx@capgemini.co.uk>> To:
         "'web-editor@kcl.ac.uk'"  <<web-editor@kcl.ac.uk>>
Subject: IP half scan
    Dear Sir,
IP address 137.73.yy.xxx resolving to xxxx.yyy.kcl.ac.uk. This
address issued an IP half scan (port scan) at  20:59 on
11/11/00 against the Swedish bank website hosted by ourselves.
As this is seen as an attempt to gain system information prior
to an attack, please investigate and respond to myself as soon
as possible with details as to who, and why this occurred. If
you are not the correct contact, please advise of the correct
contact.
    Regards
    Axxx J Sxxxx Principal Consultant & Team Leader National
Security Team Cap Gemini Telecom Media &
    Networks UK Limited External: +44 (0) 870 904 4288 DHD
Internal: 700 4288 FAX: +44 (0) 1709 846229
    E-mail: Axx.J.Sxxxx@capgemini.co.uk abc
```

Hacking does happen.

Bibliography

Hunt, C., *TCP/IP Network Administration*, O'Reilly

- This had most of the network information I needed. Access to our network team supplied the rest. There is nothing to beat talking to another human!

The following is a good place to start for help:

- http://www.linux.org/docs/ldp/howto/HOWTO-INDEX/ howtos.html

Two specific how-tos you might like to look at are:

- http://www.linux.org/docs/ldp/howto/Security-HOWTO. html
- http://www.linux.org/docs/ldp/howto/Firewall-HOWTO. html

Several versions are available. Downloading the PDF versions means that they can be looked at off-line at home.

The Secure Shell Community Site:

- http://www.ssh.org/

SuSE Linux: Security Announcements:

- http://www.suse.de/de/support/security/

Kerberos home site:

- http://web.mit.edu/kerberos/www/

Chapter

9

More Unix

The aim of this chapter is to look at some of the ways of using the commands that are part of Unix.

This chapter looks at a subset of the commands available under Unix.

Computer system overview

You should now be aware that there are several components to a complete computer system including:

- the basic hardware
- the BIOS
- the operating system

and it is possible to run more than one operating system on top of the same hardware and BIOS – you have seen an example of running three operating systems (Windows 98, SuSe 7 and Red Hat 7) on top of the same hardware and BIOS.

These operating systems offer two ways of working.

The first is via a graphical interface with icons and windows and it is interesting to see the degree of convergence that is taking place with the various flavours of both Linux and Windows.

The second is by actually typing commands in. This is done under Microsoft Windows via a DOS prompt and under Linux via a terminal window.

This chapter looks in more depth at some of these commands.

The command interpreter or shell

When we actually type things in we are interacting with the underlying computer system via a command interpreter, or shell in Unix terminology. The command interpreter under Microsoft Windows has developed considerably since the first release of the PC. Under Linux we even have the option of choosing from several shells including

- Bash – the default under both SuSe and Red Hat Linux.
- sh – the original Unix shell, also called the Bourne shell, named after the person who wrote it
- csh – the C shell, which is a shell with a syntax similar to the C programming language and developed at Berkeley.

Other shells exist including:

- ksh – the Korn shell
- tcsh – an enhanced Berkeley shell.

There are two ways of looking at the shells

- by family
  - o Bourne shell versus C shell
- by functionality
  - o the original Bourne and C shells lack command line editing.

The following table summarizes the various shell facilities.

Option/Shell	Bourne	C	TC	Korn	Bash		
Command history	No		Yes	Yes	Yes	Yes	
Command alias	No		Yes	Yes	Yes	Yes	
Shell scripts	Yes	Yes	Yes	Yes	Yes		
Filename completion	No		Yes*	Yes	Yes*	Yes	
Command line editing			No	No	Yes	Yes*	Yes
Job control	No	Yes	Yes	Yes	Yes		

The Bash shell is probably the easiest shell to use.

Basic Bash

Bash is the GNU Bourne Again Shell and is copyright the Free Software Foundation Inc. It is an sh-compatible command interpreter that executes commands read from standard input or a file. Bash also incorporates features from the Korn and C shells. It is ultimately intended to be a conformant implementation of the IEEE POSIX Shells and Tools specification – IEEE Working Group 1003.2

Before looking at Bash in any more depth we are going to cover a very important feature of Unix and that is pattern matching and the support for it within a number of Unix commands including the Bash shell.

Pattern matching

Most people will have used an editor to search for a string within a file. This will normally be done by exactly matching a sequence of characters. You will also have done replacements of one string with another in a file.

Whilst the above functionality is useful there are circumstances when we would like to do something more flexible, e.g.

- look at the beginning of a line for something
- look at the end of a line for something
- ignore the case of the text string
- match one of several strings, e.g. a title like Mr, Miss, Ms etc.

To achieve the above we need a set of metacharacters – these are characters that have special meaning within a search string. A text pattern (or regular expression) will contain a mix of ordinary characters with metacharacters.

You are already familiar with a couple of metacharacters from using file names with wild card characters, e.g.

- ls *.cxx

will list all files with a cxx file extension.

Metacharacters

The first thing we'll do is have a look at the metacharacters and then look at some simple usage.

Metacharacters and Search Pattern Examples	
.	any single character
*	match any number (including none) of the single character that precedes it
^	match at beginning of line
$	match at end of line
[ ]	match any of the enclosed characters
[^]	match any character not in the enclosed characters
[0-9]	match any digit
[A-Z]	match any upper case character
[a-z]	match any lower case character
\(\)	save the pattern (from 1 to 9) and make it available in a substitution

Search examples

The examples are based on using ex within vi.

Pattern	Match
/lan/	lan
/^lan/	lan at beginning of line
/lan$/	lan at end of line
[aeiou]	lower case vowel
[0-9]	any digit
[A-Z]	any uppercase letter

Search and replace examples

g/^$/d	delete all blank lines
1,$s/^ *//	delete leading blanks from all lines
%s/^ *//	as above.

We will now look at some actual examples using both vi and sed.

Unix metacharacters and associated programs

Metacharacters can be used in the following programs:

- awk
- ed
- egrep
- ex
- grep
- sed
- vi

and the following table summarizes the metacharacters and their associated Linux program.

Symbol/Program	awk	ed	egrep	ex	grep	sed	vi	Meaning
.	y	y	y	y	y	y	y	any
*	y	y	y	y	y	y	y	zero or more
^	y	y	y	y	y	y	y	beginning
$	y	y	y	y	y	y	y	end
\	y	y	y	y	y	y	y	escape follows
[]	y	y	y	y	y	y	y	set
\(\)		y		y		y		store for reuse
{}	y					y		range
\{\}		y	y			y		range
\<<\>>				y			y	beginning or end
+	y		y		y			one or more
?	y		y		y			zero or more
|	y		y					separate choices
()	y		y					group expressions

The best way of seeing the power of the above is with some examples.

Example 1

This example is based on compiling a suite of programs under one or more compilers. The following is a suite of Fortran 95 programs that are actual sample programs from an introductory text on programming with Fortran 95. See the reference at the end of the chapter for more details. This is generated using

- ls -la >> lsla.1

at the operating system prompt.

```
total 156
drwxrwxrwx  1 0   0        0  Dec 23  16:21 .
drwxrwxrwx  1 0   0        0  Dec 23  16:21 ..
-rwxrwxrwa  1 0   0      238  Dec 23  16:22 C0701.F90
-rwxrwxrwa  1 0   0      415  Dec 23  16:22 C0702.F90
-rwxrwxrwa  1 0   0      823  Dec 23  16:22 C0801.F90
-rwxrwxrwa  1 0   0      316  Dec 23  16:22 C0802.F90
-rwxrwxrwa  1 0   0     2114  Dec 23  16:22 C0803.F90
-rwxrwxrwa  1 0   0     1116  Dec 23  16:22 C0804.F90
-rwxrwxrwa  1 0   0      399  Dec 23  16:22 C0901.F90
-rwxrwxrwa  1 0   0      895  Dec 23  16:22 C0902.F90
-rwxrwxrwa  1 0   0      444  Dec 23  16:22 C1001.F90
-rwxrwxrwa  1 0   0      354  Dec 23  16:22 C1002.F90
-rwxrwxrwa  1 0   0      241  Dec 23  16:22 C1003.F90
-rwxrwxrwa  1 0   0      260  Dec 23  16:22 C1004.F90
-rwxrwxrwa  1 0   0      243  Dec 23  16:22 C1005.F90
-rwxrwxrwa  1 0   0      700  Dec 23  16:22 C1006.F90
-rwxrwxrwa  1 0   0      616  Dec 23  16:22 C1101.F90
-rwxrwxrwa  1 0   0     1121  Dec 23  16:22 C1102.F90
-rwxrwxrwa  1 0   0      235  Dec 23  16:22 C1201.F90
-rwxrwxrwa  1 0   0      172  Dec 23  16:22 C1401.F90
-rwxrwxrwa  1 0   0      176  Dec 23  16:22 C1402.F90
-rwxrwxrwa  1 0   0      157  Dec 23  16:22 C1403.F90
-rwxrwxrwa  1 0   0      245  Dec 23  16:22 C1404.F90
-rwxrwxrwa  1 0   0      176  Dec 23  16:22 C1405.F90
-rwxrwxrwa  1 0   0     1468  Dec 23  16:22 C1406.F90
-rwxrwxrwa  1 0   0      307  Dec 23  16:22 C1407.F90
-rwxrwxrwa  1 0   0      536  Dec 23  16:22 C1408.F90
-rwxrwxrwa  1 0   0      498  Dec 23  16:22 C1409.F90
-rwxrwxrwa  1 0   0      495  Dec 23  16:22 C1410.F90
-rwxrwxrwa  1 0   0      501  Dec 23  16:22 C1411.F90
-rwxrwxrwa  1 0   0      716  Dec 23  16:22 C1501.F90
-rwxrwxrwa  1 0   0      836  Dec 23  16:22 C1502.F90
-rwxrwxrwa  1 0   0      703  Dec 23  16:22 C1503.F90
-rwxrwxrwa  1 0   0     1222  Dec 23  16:22 C1504.F90
-rwxrwxrwa  1 0   0      552  Dec 23  16:22 C1505.F90
-rwxrwxrwa  1 0   0     1183  Dec 23  16:22 C1506.F90
-rwxrwxrwa  1 0   0      842  Dec 23  16:22 C1701.F90
-rwxrwxrwa  1 0   0      276  Dec 23  16:22 C1901.F90
-rwxrwxrwa  1 0   0      822  Dec 23  16:22 C1902.F90
-rwxrwxrwa  1 0   0     2091  Dec 23  16:22 C1903.F90
-rwxrwxrwa  1 0   0      190  Dec 23  16:22 C2001.F90
-rwxrwxrwa  1 0   0      803  Dec 23  16:22 C2002.F90
-rwxrwxrwa  1 0   0     1706  Dec 23  16:22 C2003.F90
-rwxrwxrwa  1 0   0     3724  Dec 23  16:22 C2004.F90
-rwxrwxrwa  1 0   0      352  Dec 23  16:22 C2101.F90
```

```
-rwxrwxrwa  1 0     0      244     Dec 23  16:22  C2102.F90
-rwxrwxrwa  1 0     0      778     Dec 23  16:22  C2103.F90
-rwxrwxrwa  1 0     0      1983    Dec 23  16:22  C2201.F90
-rwxrwxrwa  1 0     0      724     Dec 23  16:22  C2301.F90
-rwxrwxrwa  1 0     0      701     Dec 23  16:22  C2302.F90
-rwxrwxrwa  1 0     0      4528    Dec 23  16:22  C2303.F90
-rwxrwxrwa  1 0     0      943     Dec 23  16:22  C2304.F90
-rwxrwxrwa  1 0     0      227     Dec 23  16:22  C2305.F90
-rwxrwxrwa  1 0     0      640     Dec 23  16:22  C2401.F90
-rwxrwxrwa  1 0     0      1109    Dec 23  16:22  C2402.F90
-rwxrwxrwa  1 0     0      2122    Dec 23  16:22  C2403.F90
-rwxrwxrwa  1 0     0      1067    Dec 23  16:22  C2404.F90
-rwxrwxrwa  1 0     0      3796    Dec 23  16:22  C2405.F90
-rwxrwxrwa  1 0     0      4696    Dec 23  16:22  C2601.F90
-rwxrwxrwa  1 0     0      6055    Dec 23  16:22  C2602.F90
-rwxrwxrwa  1 0     0      1744    Dec 23  16:22  C2603.F90
-rwxrwxrwa  1 0     0      676     Dec 23  16:22  C2604.F90
-rwxrwxrwa  1 0     0      263     Dec 24  10:30  c1202.f90
-rwxrwxrwa  1 0     0      0       Dec 28  14:43  lsla.1
```

The key things to note are:

- ls generates a sorted list
- all but two of the files have C as the first character of the file name
- all but two of the files have F as the first character of the file name extension
- Linux and Unix file names are case sensitive.

We are interested in generating the following line for each program that has to be compiled:

- f95 c1001.f90 -o c1001.out 2>c1001.lst

and we look at each option in turn

- f95 – invoke the Fortran 95 compiler
- c1001.f90 – file to compile
- -o c1001.out – write the executable to c1001.out
- 2>c1001.lst – write any compilation error messages to c1001.lst.

So what we need to do is convert each line from using ls -la into one similar to the above. We need to:

- delete all lines that aren't Fortran source code

- convert the lower case example to upper case
- remove everything from the line except the file name
- rename the files to have lower case file names – the file names originated on a PC where case doesn't matter
- convert the file name into three file names
- convert each respective file name to have the correct file name extension
- insert the f95 command on each line
- insert the -o option on each line
- redirect the error messages to the corresponding file name.

We will do this in two stages. The first will convert to lower case and the second will do the rest. We will be doing this in so-called batch mode where we use a small script for sed to do the work.

Lower case file names

This is the sed script that renames the files to lower case.

```
/^total/d
/^d/d
/lsla/d
s/ c/ C/
s/^..* C/C/
s/\(..*\)/\1 \1/
s/ C/ c/
s/\.F90$/\.f90/
s/^/mv /
```

We will look at each line in turn and explain what it is doing:

- /^total/d
  - delete each line with the string total on it
- /^d/d
  - delete each line beginning with d – i.e. is a directory
- /lsla/d
  - delete each line that has the string lsla on it
- s/ c/ C/
  - convert the one lower case file name to upper case
- s/^..* C/C/
  - remove everything on the line except the file name

- s/\(..*\)/\1 \1/
  - o duplicate the file name
- s/ C/ c/
  - o convert all occurrences of space upper case c to space lower case c
- s/\.F90$/\.f90/
  - o replace the string .F90 end of line with .f90
- s/^/mv /
  - o add the rename command to the beginning of each line.

The output from sed is then written to the file that will actually do the file name renaming. This is done by typing

- sed -f lower.sed lsla.1 > lower.bat

and we will look at each component of this line in turn:

- sed – invoke sed
- -f lower.sed – read the sed script from the file named lower.sed
- lsla.1 – the sed input file to process
- > lower.bat – write the output to the file called lower.bat.

This will create the file called

- lower.bat

and you need to make this file executable by typing

- chmod +x lower.bat

which changes the mode (chmod) of the file to executable (+x) and actually typing

- lower.bat

will rename all of the files. We next look at creating the compile file. We need to type

- ls -la > lsla.2

to create the new sed input file for stage two. We will now be working with lower case file names. We will be creating a file called compile.sed which is the sed script to do the work. This is given opposite:

```
/^total/d
/^d/d
/compile/d
/lsla/d
/lower/d
s/^..* c/c/
s/\(..*\)/\1 -o \1# 2> \1/
s/\.f90#/\.out/
s/\.f90$/\.lis/
s/^/f95 /
```

and we will look at each line in turn:

- /^total/d
  - ○ delete all lines with total on them
- /^d/d
  - ○ delete all lines that start with the letter d – are directories not files
- /compile/d
  - ○ delete all lines that have compile on them – the sed script that is this file
- /lsla/d
  - ○ delete all lines with lsla on them
- /lower/d
  - ○ delete all lines with lower on them
- s/^..* c/c/
  - ○ remove all but the file names from each line
- s/\(..*\)/\1 -o \1# 2>> \1/
  - ○ replace one file name with three file names adding the output file name and error listing options
- s/\.f90#/\.out/
  - ○ replace the middle file name extension (marked by adding the hash character) with the appropriate output file name extension for the executable
- s/\.f90$/\.lis/
  - ○ replace the last file name extension on the line (using the $ metacharacter that means end of line) with the error listing output file name extension
- s/^/f95 /
  - ○ add the actual compiler name at the beginning of each line.

Typing

- sed -f compile.sed lsla.2 >> compile.bat

creates the following file

```
f95  c0701.f90  -o  c0701.out  2>>  c0701.lis
f95  c0702.f90  -o  c0702.out  2>>  c0702.lis
f95  c0801.f90  -o  c0801.out  2>>  c0801.lis
f95  c0802.f90  -o  c0802.out  2>>  c0802.lis
f95  c0803.f90  -o  c0803.out  2>>  c0803.lis
f95  c0804.f90  -o  c0804.out  2>>  c0804.lis
f95  c0901.f90  -o  c0901.out  2>>  c0901.lis
f95  c0902.f90  -o  c0902.out  2>>  c0902.lis
f95  c1001.f90  -o  c1001.out  2>>  c1001.lis
f95  c1002.f90  -o  c1002.out  2>>  c1002.lis
f95  c1003.f90  -o  c1003.out  2>>  c1003.lis
f95  c1004.f90  -o  c1004.out  2>>  c1004.lis
f95  c1005.f90  -o  c1005.out  2>>  c1005.lis
f95  c1006.f90  -o  c1006.out  2>>  c1006.lis
f95  c1101.f90  -o  c1101.out  2>>  c1101.lis
f95  c1102.f90  -o  c1102.out  2>>  c1102.lis
f95  c1201.f90  -o  c1201.out  2>>  c1201.lis
f95  c1202.f90  -o  c1202.out  2>>  c1202.lis
f95  c1401.f90  -o  c1401.out  2>>  c1401.lis
f95  c1402.f90  -o  c1402.out  2>>  c1402.lis
f95  c1403.f90  -o  c1403.out  2>>  c1403.lis
f95  c1404.f90  -o  c1404.out  2>>  c1404.lis
f95  c1405.f90  -o  c1405.out  2>>  c1405.lis
f95  c1406.f90  -o  c1406.out  2>>  c1406.lis
f95  c1407.f90  -o  c1407.out  2>>  c1407.lis
f95  c1408.f90  -o  c1408.out  2>>  c1408.lis
f95  c1409.f90  -o  c1409.out  2>>  c1409.lis
f95  c1410.f90  -o  c1410.out  2>>  c1410.lis
f95  c1411.f90  -o  c1411.out  2>>  c1411.lis
f95  c1501.f90  -o  c1501.out  2>>  c1501.lis
f95  c1502.f90  -o  c1502.out  2>>  c1502.lis
f95  c1503.f90  -o  c1503.out  2>>  c1503.lis
f95  c1504.f90  -o  c1504.out  2>>  c1504.lis
f95  c1505.f90  -o  c1505.out  2>>  c1505.lis
f95  c1506.f90  -o  c1506.out  2>>  c1506.lis
f95  c1701.f90  -o  c1701.out  2>>  c1701.lis
f95  c1901.f90  -o  c1901.out  2>>  c1901.lis
f95  c1902.f90  -o  c1902.out  2>>  c1902.lis
f95  c1903.f90  -o  c1903.out  2>>  c1903.lis
f95  c2001.f90  -o  c2001.out  2>>  c2001.lis
f95  c2002.f90  -o  c2002.out  2>>  c2002.lis
```

```
f95 c2003.f90 -o c2003.out 2>> c2003.lis
f95 c2004.f90 -o c2004.out 2>> c2004.lis
f95 c2101.f90 -o c2101.out 2>> c2101.lis
f95 c2102.f90 -o c2102.out 2>> c2102.lis
f95 c2103.f90 -o c2103.out 2>> c2103.lis
f95 c2201.f90 -o c2201.out 2>> c2201.lis
f95 c2301.f90 -o c2301.out 2>> c2301.lis
f95 c2302.f90 -o c2302.out 2>> c2302.lis
f95 c2303.f90 -o c2303.out 2>> c2303.lis
f95 c2304.f90 -o c2304.out 2>> c2304.lis
f95 c2305.f90 -o c2305.out 2>> c2305.lis
f95 c2401.f90 -o c2401.out 2>> c2401.lis
f95 c2402.f90 -o c2402.out 2>> c2402.lis
f95 c2403.f90 -o c2403.out 2>> c2403.lis
f95 c2404.f90 -o c2404.out 2>> c2404.lis
f95 c2405.f90 -o c2405.out 2>> c2405.lis
f95 c2601.f90 -o c2601.out 2>> c2601.lis
f95 c2602.f90 -o c2602.out 2>> c2602.lis
f95 c2603.f90 -o c2603.out 2>> c2603.lis
f95 c2604.f90 -o c2604.out 2>> c2604.lis
```

and typing

- chmod +x compile.bat

creates the executable file that will compile each of the programs writing the executable file and error files to the appropriate files. If there are any compilation warnings the .lst files will have a non-zero size. These files can be printed using

- xargs ls *.lst | pr {} {}

and this will add a header and footer with the file name to the printout making it very easy to see what the compilation error messages are.

A similar process can be followed for compiling other source files including C++ and Java.

Example 2

This example looks at creating a mailing list from a course booking system. The default output from this system is given below.

```
                Computing Centre Course List

course-code : d5-1-autumn99
status      : Confirmed
last-name   : alexiou
first-name  : maria
category    : pg(t)
cc-id       : kkma5258
phone       : unknown
email       : maria.alexiou@kcl.ac.uk
department  : dentistry
school      : kcsmd

course-code : d5-1-autumn99
status      : Confirmed
last-name   : begent
first-name  : louise
category    : pg(r)
cc-id       : khva1418
phone       : 4797
email       : louise.begent@kcl.ac.uk
department  : pharmacy
school      : life sciences

course-code : d5-1-autumn99
status      : Confirmed
last-name   : charon
first-name  : celine
category    : stf
cc-id       : stma0227
phone       : 848 4822/848 4877
email       : celine.charon@kcl.ac.uk
department  : pharmacy
school      : life sciences

course-code : d5-1-autumn99
status      : Confirmed
last-name   : clarke
first-name  : helen
category    : pg(r)
cc-id       : zmmk2505
phone       : 4024
email       : helen.clarke@kcl.ac.uk
department  : renal medicine
school      : kcsmd
```

```
course-code  : d5-1-autumn99
status       : Confirmed
last-name    : epelle
first-name   : ibelema
category     : pg(t)
cc-id        : kkjd3481
phone        : 0961389780
email        : ibelema.epelle@kcl.ac.uk
department   : pharmacy
school       : life sciences

course-code  : d5-1-autumn99
status       : Confirmed
last-name    : hansen
first-name   : anne
category     : pg(r)
cc-id        : kfba8717
phone        : 4501
email        : anne.hansen@kcl.ac.uk
department   : life sciences
school       : life sciences

course-code  : d5-1-autumn99
status       : Confirmed
last-name    : pouria
first-name   : shideh
category     : pg(r)
cc-id        : zmmk2224
phone        : 72-4837
email        : shideh.pouria@kcl.ac.uk
department   : renal medicine
school       : kcsmd

course-code  : d5-1-autumn99
status       : Confirmed
last-name    : tischkowitz
first-name   : marc
category     : stf
cc-id        : stma0315
phone        : 955 4648
email        : marc.d.tischkowitz@kcl.ac.uk
department   : all departments
school       : umds

course-code  : d5-1-autumn99
status       : Withdrawn
```

```
last-name    : chaturvedi
first-name   : rajiv
category     : pg(r)
cc-id        : kkma6754
phone        : unknown
email        : rajiv.chaturvedi@kcl.ac.uk
department   : molecular biology & biophysics
school       : life sciences
```

The key thing to note here are is that we are only interested in the lines containing the string email. We need to delete every other line.

The sed file that solves this is given below.

```
/^ /d
/^$/d
/course-code/d
/status/d
/last-name/d
/first-name/d
/category/d
/cc-id/d
/phone/d
/department/d
/school/d
s/email       : //
s/$/ ,/
```

The first line deletes any line starting with a blank. The second deletes any blank line. The last line adds a comma at the end of each line. This is required by the email package.

The output from running sed is given below.

```
maria.alexiou@kcl.ac.uk ,
louise.begent@kcl.ac.uk ,
celine.charon@kcl.ac.uk ,
helen.clarke@kcl.ac.uk ,
ibelema.epelle@kcl.ac.uk ,
anne.hansen@kcl.ac.uk ,
shideh.pouria@kcl.ac.uk ,
marc.d.tischkowitz@kcl.ac.uk ,
rajiv.chaturvedi@kcl.ac.uk ,
```

The last trailing comma was deleted in vi.

Working with files, directories and the file system

It is possible to do a lot from the file manager. Now we will look under the hood at the Unix file system.

Typing

- pwd

will show you where you currently are within the file system.

The following is an example of typing:

- ls -la

in the home directory under Red Hat Linux 6.2

```
total 33700
drwx------ 21 sttp1553 sttp1553    4096 Jan 16 12:21 .
drwxr-xr-x  6 root     root        4096 Aug 30 20:04 ..
-rw-------  1 sttp1553 sttp1553    3689 Jan 16 12:15 .ICEauthority
-rw-------  1 sttp1553 sttp1553     105 Jan 16 12:15 .Xauthority
-rwxr-xr-x  1 sttp1553 sttp1553     188 Dec  5 16:34 .Xclients
-rwxr-xr-x  1 sttp1553 sttp1553      57 Dec  5 17:09 .Xclients-default
-rw-rw-r--  1 sttp1553 sttp1553       0 Jan 10 16:17 .addressbook
-rw-------  1 sttp1553 sttp1553    2285 Jan 10 16:17 .addressbook.lu
-rw-------  1 sttp1553 sttp1553    7452 Jan 15 18:49 .bash_history
-rw-r--r--  1 sttp1553 sttp1553      24 Aug 30 20:04 .bash_logout
-rw-r--r--  1 sttp1553 sttp1553     230 Aug 30 20:04 .bash_profile
-rw-r--r--  1 sttp1553 sttp1553     124 Aug 30 20:04 .bashrc
drwx------  2 sttp1553 sttp1553    4096 Jan 10 17:46 .elm
-rwxr-xr-x  1 sttp1553 sttp1553     333 Aug 30 20:04 .emacs
drwx------  3 sttp1553 sttp1553    4096 Jan 16 12:15 .enlightenment
drwxr-xr-x  6 sttp1553 sttp1553    4096 Jan 16 12:16 .gnome
drwxrwxr-x  2 sttp1553 sttp1553    4096 Dec 12 17:15 .gnome-desktop
drwxr-xr-x  2 sttp1553 sttp1553    4096 Sep  1  5:55 .gnome-help-browser
drwx------  2 sttp1553 sttp1553    4096 Aug 31 15:09 .gnome_private
drwxrwxr-x  2 sttp1553 sttp1553    4096 Oct 26 17:31 .gnp
drwxr-xr-x  3 sttp1553 sttp1553    4096 Aug 30 20:04 .kde
-rw-r--r--  1 sttp1553 sttp1553     665 Dec  5 17:03 .kderc
drwxrwxr-x  2 sttp1553 sttp1553    4096 Dec 12 17:13 .mc
drwxrwxr-x  5 sttp1553 sttp1553    4096 Dec  5 16:26 .netscape
-rw-rw-r--  1 sttp1553 sttp1553   13738 Jan 10 16:17 .pinerc
-rw-r--r--  1 sttp1553 sttp1553    3394 Aug 30 20:04 .screenrc
```

```
drwx------   3 sttp1553 sttp1553     4096 Aug 31 15:13 .xauth
-rw-------   1 sttp1553 sttp1553      360 Jan 16 12:16 .xsession-errors
drwxr-xr-x   5 sttp1553 sttp1553     4096 Aug 30 20:04 Desktop
drwxrwxr-x   5 sttp1553 sttp1553     4096 Sep 26 16:38 ILINXR.install
drwx------   2 sttp1553 sttp1553     4096 Jan 10 17:52 Mail
-rwxrwxr-x   1 sttp1553 sttp1553   185014 Oct 31 12:13 a.out
-rw-r--r--   1 sttp1553 sttp1553      104 Oct 31 12:13 c06eafe.d
-rw-r--r--   1 sttp1553 sttp1553     2058 Oct 31 12:13 c06eafe.f
-rw-rw-r--   1 sttp1553 sttp1553        0 Dec  5 16:16 chap05gnome01.jpg
-rw-rw-r--   1 sttp1553 sttp1553  2922149 Dec  5 16:17 chap05gnome01.ps
drwxrwxr-x   2 sttp1553 sttp1553     4096 Oct 17 19:14 cxx
-rw-------   1 sttp1553 sttp1553      424 Jan 12 18:12 dead.letter
-rw-rw-r--   1 sttp1553 sttp1553   323448 Oct 12 18:00 dns.txt
-rw-rw-r--   1 sttp1553 sttp1553     5845 Dec 12 13:27 du.k
-rw-rw-r--   1 sttp1553 sttp1553     5436 Jan 10 17:47 elmredhat.gif
-rw-rw-r--   1 sttp1553 sttp1553     3834 Jan 10 17:47 elmredhat.png
-rw-rw-r--   1 sttp1553 sttp1553  1073453 Jan 10 17:47 elmredhat.ps
-rw-rw-r--   1 sttp1553 sttp1553   364461 Sep 25 16:28 fhs-2.1.pdf
-rw-rw-r--   1 sttp1553 sttp1553        0 Dec  5 16:29 gnorpm01.jpg
-rw-rw-r--   1 sttp1553 sttp1553    20009 Sep  4 16:46 hosts.allow
-rw-rw-r--   1 sttp1553 sttp1553     3029 Sep  6 15:35 inetd.conf
-rw-rw-r--   1 sttp1553 sttp1553 15946240 Sep 25 17:33 linux-ar-405.tar
-rw-rw-r--   1 sttp1553 sttp1553        0 Jan 16 12:21 lsla.redhat6
drwx------   2 sttp1553 sttp1553     4096 Jan 10 17:30 mail
-rw-rw-r--   1 sttp1553 sttp1553     8103 Jan 10 17:33 mailredhat
-rw-rw-r--   1 sttp1553 sttp1553    11060 Jan 10 17:33 mailredhat.gif
-rw-rw-r--   1 sttp1553 sttp1553  1171705 Jan 10 17:33 mailredhat.ps
-rw-------   1 sttp1553 sttp1553     2521 Jan 12 16:58 mbox
-rw-rw-r--   1 sttp1553 sttp1553  1710630 Sep 13 16:38 nag-1.0.pdf
drwxrwxr-x   4 sttp1553 sttp1553     4096 Oct 17 11:56 nagf95
drwxrwxr-x   3 root     root         4096 Sep 25 16:36 naglib
-rw-r--r--   1 root     root       312604 Sep 13 17:55 nslookup.txt
drwx------   2 sttp1553 sttp1553     4096 Aug 31 15:14 nsmail
-rw-rw-r--   1 sttp1553 sttp1553    12844 Sep 18 14:17 packages.redhat
-rw-rw-r--   1 sttp1553 sttp1553     9449 Jan 10 17:36 pineredhat.gif
-rw-rw-r--   1 sttp1553 sttp1553     6375 Jan 10 17:36 pineredhat.png
-rw-rw-r--   1 sttp1553 sttp1553  1171705 Jan 10 17:44 pineredhat.ps
-rw-rw-r--   1 sttp1553 sttp1553     3782 Jan 12 16:59 psef.silverbirch
-rw-rw-r--   1 sttp1553 sttp1553   817284 Oct 30 17:51 redhat.1
-rw-rw-r--   1 sttp1553 sttp1553     1302 Sep 18 16:46 redhat.fhs
-rw-rw-r--   1 sttp1553 sttp1553     1468 Sep 18 17:46 redhat.usr
-rw-rw-r--   1 sttp1553 sttp1553     3624 Jan 12 13:32 redhat6.varlog
-rw-rw-r--   1 sttp1553 sttp1553    24056 Jan 12 13:30 redhathelp01.gif
-rw-rw-r--   1 sttp1553 sttp1553    14648 Jan 12 13:30 redhathelp01.png
-rw-rw-r--   1 sttp1553 sttp1553  2922150 Jan 12 13:30 redhathelp01.ps
-rw-rw-r--   1 sttp1553 sttp1553    12844 Dec 12 13:24 rpm_list.txt
```

```
-rw-rw-r—  1 sttp1553 sttp1553  308329 Sep 13 16:37 sag-0.6.2.pdf
-rw-rw-r—  1 sttp1553 sttp1553   17777 Sep  6 11:32 sendmail.txt
-rw-rw-r—  1 sttp1553 sttp1553    1780 Oct 26 17:12 set.txt
-rw-rw-r—  1 sttp1553 sttp1553   12844 Dec 12 16:05 sorted_rpm_list.txt
-rw-rw-r—  1 sttp1553 sttp1553 1154554 Sep 13 16:36 user-beta-1.pdf.zip
-rw-rw-r—  1 sttp1553 sttp1553   10013 Jan 10 17:54 xmailer.gif
-rw-rw-r—  1 sttp1553 sttp1553    6174 Jan 10 17:54 xmailer.png
-rw-rw-r—  1 sttp1553 sttp1553 2922150 Jan 10 17:55 xmailer.ps
-rw-rw-r—  1 root     root      323481 Oct 13 16:15 z.z
-rw-rw-r—  1 sttp1553 sttp1553  324290 Nov 14 14:34 zz.zz
-rw-rw-r—  1 sttp1553 sttp1553   13651 Dec 12 16:08 zzz.zzz
```

Let us look at each component of this information in turn.

The first character in the above example is either

- d

or

- -

d means directory, and – means a normal file.

The next 9 characters are interpreted as three sets of information organized as

- owner permissions
- group permissions
- world permissions

and the permissions are

- r – the file is readable
- w – the file is writable
- x – the file is executable
- - – the indicated permission is not granted.

For a directory, execute permission allows access to file names within that directory. This is useful if you want people to see what files you have and possibly read them or copy them.

The second column indicates the number of links to the file. Look at the so-called system or hidden files at the start of this listing. Some of these have several links to them. This means that several components of the system use these files to determine what they should do. This means that you can alter the default behaviour of Linux and Unix systems by making changes to these files.

The next two indicate

- owner
- group

respectively. If you look at the entries for naglib and nslookup you will see that they do not belong to the user sttp1553. They belong to root. This is because I did some installation work for the library as root, but did it in this user's directory. The user can't delete these files.

Finally we have

- size
- date and time information
- file name.

Have a look at the system you have and see how things are organized. Some of the commands to work with the file system include

- cd – change directory
- mkdir – make directory
- pwd – print out where you are within the directory structure
- ls – display the files
- cp – copy files
- mv – rename files
- chmod – change the mode of a file
- find – locate files within a directory tree

and you've seen examples of the above throughout the notes as and when they were required.

Help

So far we've looked at a variety of ways of getting help. These have included the on-line help systems available within a graphical environment and also what can be done by actually typing commands in with

- apropos
- man
- info.

info provides probably the most readable source of information from the command line.

vi

vi has been installed on every Unix and Linux system I've ever worked with. I strongly recommend getting familiar with using it. The investment in your time will eventually pay off big time.

The home page for the enhanced version vim, which is aimed at programmers, can be found at:

- http://www.linux.org/docs/ldp/howto/Vim-HOWTO. html

We will look at basic vi in this chapter. There are three modes to vi:

- screen mode
- insert text mode
- command mode

and it is convenient to think of this as having the ability to switch between

- screen mode to insert mode and back again
- screen mode to command mode and back again.

The basic commands to switch between the modes are

- screen mode to insert mode – i or a
- insert mode to screen mode – [esc]
- screen mode to command mode – :
- command mode to screen mode – [return]

Notes

Only the two most common modes for going between screen mode to insert mode are given above. The full list is given later.

You can switch automatically between command mode and screen mode simply by pressing the [return] key at the end of the commands you want executed.

If things don't go as expected you are probably in insert mode and have forgotten to press the [escape] key.

Starting and ending vi

To start vi type

- vi filename

at the shell prompt. There are a number of ways of leaving vi and some of the most common are:

- :wq – save and exit (write and quit)
- :w – save
- :w newfile – save to newfile
- :e! – discard changes and start again with the original file
- :q! – exit without saving
- ZZ – quick save and exit.

The vi modes

It seems a little strange at first that vi has three modes of use and that you can't simply use the keys that you are familiar with to move around the file and screen and insert and delete text. Quite frankly it is arcane. However, eventually you will get proficient.

Screen mode – moving round the file

The arrow keys can be used for short movements – they may not work on all systems and the alternatives are also given.

↑	k	up
↓	j	down
←	h	left
→	l	right
[return]		next line
[space]		right
^		beginning of line
$		end of line
w W b B		forward/backward word at a time
[CTRL]F		forward a screen
[CTRL]B		backward a screen
1G		top of file
G		bottom of file.

Screen mode – deleting text

x	delete character
dw	delete word
dd	delete line
10dd	delete 10 lines
D	delete to end of line.

Screen mode – copying and moving text

There is the concept of buffers with vi, and you can cut and paste text between one or more buffers and the screen and vice versa.

dd	delete or cut current line into the buffer
Y	yank or copy current line into the buffer
10Y	copy the next 10 lines into the buffer
P	paste or insert the buffer before this line
p	paste or insert the buffer after this line.

Input mode

A number of keys take you into input mode. Remember to press the escape key to exit this mode!

i	insert before cursor
a	insert after cursor
I	insert at start of line
A	insert at end of line
O	insert line before current line
o	insert line after current line
R	replace text – overwrite mode
cw	change word
ncw	change n words
C	change line from cursor to end of line
S	replace whole line with input
s	replace current character with input.

Command mode

The command-driven editor is called ex. This editor is very powerful and can make trivial some of the most complex editing tasks. The shell also offers very powerful capabilities. We will not cover the shell here.

There are four characters that are used, and these are

/	search forward
?	search backward
:	invoke an ex command
!	invoke the shell.

Command mode search examples

Note that searching is case sensitive.

/lan	search for lan
?lan	search backwards for lan
/	repeat last search
?	repeat last backwards search.

Command mode – invoke ex

The basic syntax to execute an ex command from vi is

:[address] command [options]

[address] is the line number or range of lines that are to be the object of the command. Here are some address options:

1,10	from first to tenth line
1,$	from first to last
1,.	from first to current
.,.+10	from current to current + 10
.,$	from current to last.

A range of commands is available but the most useful is

s	substitute.

The most common option is a count figure.

Here are some examples:

:1,$s/string1/string2/

This will replace occurrences of string1 with string2 from the first to the last line in the file. The surprise for the beginner is that it will only replace the first occurrence on a line. Any other occurrences are left alone.

:1,$s/string1/string2/999

As above but now replace up to 999 occurrences on any line.

The real power of the substitute command becomes apparent when combined with pattern matching. Some of the special characters used are:

^	anchor to beginning of line
$	anchor to end of line
.	any character
*	zero or more matches of the previous pattern
[]	used to define a set of characters.

Let us look at some examples now:

1,$s/ *$//	1,$ apply the command to every line in the file. s substitute / *$/ all trailing blanks // replace with nothing.

So the above command will get rid of all the trailing blanks on a line.

1,$s/^ *//   strip off all leading blanks

There is another command that proves very useful and the syntax of this command is:

g/pattern/command

and an example of the power of this command is given below:

g/^$/d

This command will mark each line in the file that matches the pattern in the // – in this case each line that is a blank line, and delete it.

Here are some other pattern examples:

/a.c/	match a followed by any character and then a c.
/[0-9][0-9]/	match any line with a 2 digit number in it.

It is not possible in such a short coverage to show the full power of what vi can do. Hopefully this will have whetted your appetite!

Managing jobs and processes

When you type in a command or click on an icon it invokes a program. While this program is running it is called a process. Let us look now at running the following command

* ps -ef

and having a look at the output. The following is taken from a Red Hat system.

```
UID      PID PPID C STIME TTY    TIME       CMD
root       1    0 0 11:29 ?      00:00:05 init [5]
root       2    1 0 11:29 ?      00:00:01 [kflushd]
root       3    1 0 11:29 ?      00:00:00 [kupdate]
root       4    1 0 11:29 ?      00:00:00 [kpiod]
root       5    1 0 11:29 ?      00:00:05 [kswapd]
root       6    1 0 11:29 ?      00:00:00 [mdrecoveryd]
bin      353    1 0 11:30 ?      00:00:00 [portmap]
root     368    1 0 11:30 ?      00:00:00 [lockd]
root     369  368 0 11:30 ?      00:00:00 [rpciod]
root     378    1 0 11:30 ?      00:00:00 [rpc.statd]
root     407    1 0 11:30 ?      00:00:00 /usr/sbin/automount —timeout 60
root     460    1 0 11:30 ?      00:00:00 syslogd -m 0
root     469    1 0 11:30 ?      00:00:01 klogd
nobody   483    1 0 11:30 ?      00:00:00 [identd]
nobody   486  483 0 11:30 ?      00:00:00 [identd]
nobody   487  486 0 11:30 ?      00:00:00 [identd]
nobody   489  486 0 11:30 ?      00:00:00 [identd]
nobody   490  486 0 11:30 ?      00:00:00 [identd]
daemon   501    1 0 11:30 ?      00:00:00 /usr/sbin/atd
root     515    1 0 11:30 ?      00:00:00 crond
root     533    1 0 11:30 ?      00:00:00 inetd
root     547    1 0 11:30 ?      00:00:00 [lpd]
```

```
root     588      1 0 11:30 ttyS1 00:00:00 gpm -t ms
root     602      1 0 11:30 ?     00:00:04 httpd
nobody   636    602 0 11:30 ?     00:00:00 [httpd]
nobody   637    602 0 11:30 ?     00:00:00 [httpd]
nobody   638    602 0 11:30 ?     00:00:00 [httpd]
nobody   639    602 0 11:30 ?     00:00:00 [httpd]
nobody   641    602 0 11:30 ?     00:00:00 [httpd]
nobody   642    602 0 11:30 ?     00:00:00 [httpd]
nobody   643    602 0 11:30 ?     00:00:00 [httpd]
nobody   644    602 0 11:30 ?     00:00:00 [httpd]
xfs      681      1 0 11:30 ?     00:00:23 xfs -droppriv -daemon -port -1
root     721      1 0 11:30 tty1  00:00:00 [mingetty]
root     722      1 0 11:30 tty2  00:00:00 [mingetty]
root     723      1 0 11:30 tty3  00:00:00 [mingetty]
root     724      1 0 11:30 tty4  00:00:00 [mingetty]
root     725      1 0 11:30 tty5  00:00:00 [mingetty]
root     726      1 0 11:30 tty6  00:00:00 [mingetty]
root     727      1 0 11:30 ?     00:00:00 /usr/bin/gdm -nodaemon
root    1277    727 1 17:25 ?     00:00:17 /etc/X11/X -auth /var/gdm/:0.Xau
root    1278    727 0 17:25 ?     00:00:00 /usr/bin/gdm -nodaemon
sttp1553 1289  1278 0 17:26 ?     00:00:02 gnome-session
sttp1553 1327     1 0 17:26 ?     00:00:00 gnome-smproxy —sm-client-id def
sttp1553 1333     1 0 17:26 ?     00:00:05 enlightenment -clientId default2
sttp1553 1335     1 0 17:26 ?     00:00:01 magicdev —sm-client-id=default1
sttp1553 1348     1 0 17:26 ?     00:00:00 gnome-name-service
sttp1553 1350     1 0 17:26 ?     00:00:05 panel —sm-client-id default8
sttp1553 1352     1 0 17:26 ?     00:00:00 xscreensaver -no-splash -timeout
sttp1553 1354     1 0 17:26 ?     00:00:04 gmc —sm-client-id default10
sttp1553 1356     1 0 17:26 ?     00:00:04 gnome-help-browser —sm-client-i
sttp1553 1366     1 0 17:26 ?     00:00:02 gnomepager_applet —activate-goa
sttp1553 1368     1 0 17:26 ?     00:00:01 gen_util_applet —activate-goad-
sttp1553 1372     1 0 17:27 ?     00:00:02 gnome-terminal
sttp1553 1373  1372 0 17:27 ?     00:00:00 gnome-pty-helper
sttp1553 1374  1372 0 17:27 pts/0 00:00:00 bash
sttp1553 1413   533 0 17:41 ?     00:00:00 ftpd: ichivers.cc.kcl.ac.uk: stt
sttp1553 1422  1374 0 17:44 pts/0 00:00:00 ps -ef
```

Some of the columns are described below:

- UID – user id or owner
- PID – process id
- PPID – parent process id
- STIME – start time
- TTY – the controlling terminal associated with this process; a ? indicates that there is no controlling process

- TIME – the amount of CPU time used by this process
- CMD – actual command.

There are several commands that allow you to manage the processes that belong to you. You cannot do anything with processes belonging to other users. Type

- top

to see the top processes running. The following is from a Red Hat system.

```
 5:50pm  up  6:21,  2 users,  load average: 0.00, 0.00, 0.05
57 processes: 56 sleeping, 1 running, 0 zombie, 0 stopped
CPU states:  2.9% user,  1.2% system,  0.0% nice, 95.8% idle
Mem: 30632K av,  29804K used,   828K free,  31040K shrd,  724K buff
Swap:66488K av,   9504K used,  56984K free   10392K cached
PID  USER    PRI  NI SIZE RSS SHARE STAT LIB %CPU %MEM TIME  COMMAND
1428 sttp1553 12   0  840  840 648    R    0  14.1 2.7  0:00  top
1    root      0   0  108   52  40    S    0   0.0 0.1  0:05  init
2    root      0   0    0    0   0    SW   0   0.0 0.0  0:01  kflushd
3    root      0   0    0    0   0    SW   0   0.0 0.0  0:00  kupdate
4    root      0   0    0    0   0    SW   0   0.0 0.0  0:00  kpiod
5    root      0   0    0    0   0    SW   0   0.0 0.0  0:05  kswapd
6    root    -20 -20    0    0   0    SW<< 0   0.0 0.0  0:00  mdrecoveryd
353  bin       0   0   88    0   0    SW   0   0.0 0.0  0:00  portmap
368  root      0   0    0    0   0    SW   0   0.0 0.0  0:00  lockd
369  root      0   0    0    0   0    SW   0   0.0 0.0  0:00  rpciod
378  root      0   0   88    0   0    SW   0   0.0 0.0  0:00  rpc.statd
407  root      0   0  128   44  28    S    0   0.0 0.1  0:00  automount
460  root      0   0  216  168 140    S    0   0.0 0.5  0:00  syslogd
469  root      0   0  500  172 140    S    0   0.0 0.5  0:01  klogd
483  nobody    0   0  132   44  40    S    0   0.0 0.1  0:00  identd
486  nobody    0   0  132   44  40    S    0   0.0 0.1  0:00  identd
487  nobody    0   0  132   44  40    S    0   0.0 0.1  0:00  identd
```

This shows quite a lot of information about your system including

- the number of processes
- the states they are in
- the CPU state
- the memory on the system and its usage
- the swap space on your system and usage
- the priority of the processes
- the memory size of the processes

to name just a few.

Try the following on your system:

- login graphically
- start two terminal sessions
- within one of them type
  - top
- within the other type
  - netscape &

The & character means start the process (in this case Netscape) in the background. Eventually you will have two terminal windows open and Netscape. Have a look at the terminal window running top to see what is happening. Some programs take a long time to start up and Netscape is one of them. It is also quite resource hungry.

Now switch to the second terminal window and type

- kill netscape_pid

where netscape_pid is the process id of netscape. This will terminate Netscape. If a process is consuming too many resources or has hung, using kill is very effective.

The above illustrates the multitasking nature of Linux and Unix systems quite well.

Managing your environment

Your working environment is defined whenever you login or start another shell. This environment is set using the values that the shell finds in initialization files which it always reads as it starts up.

You can change your working environment by editing these files and setting new values for variables. The following is the output from

- ls -la

on a Red Hat system. It has been edited to only show the hidden files.

```
-rw-------  1 sttp1553 sttp1553 3858 Jan 19 17:26 .ICEauthority
-rw-------  1 sttp1553 sttp1553  105 Jan 19 17:26 .Xauthority
-rwxr-xr-x  1 sttp1553 sttp1553  188 Dec  5 16:34 .Xclients
-rwxr-xr-x  1 sttp1553 sttp1553   57 Dec  5 17:09 .Xclients-default
-rw-rw-r--  1 sttp1553 sttp1553    0 Jan 10 16:17 .addressbook
-rw-------  1 sttp1553 sttp1553 2285 Jan 10 16:17 .addressbook.lu
-rw-------  1 sttp1553 sttp1553 7895 Jan 19 14:49 .bash_history
-rw-r--r--  1 sttp1553 sttp1553   24 Aug 30 20:04 .bash_logout
-rw-r--r--  1 sttp1553 sttp1553  230 Aug 30 20:04 .bash_profile
-rw-r--r--  1 sttp1553 sttp1553  124 Aug 30 20:04 .bashrc
drwx------  4 sttp1553 sttp1553 4096 Jan 16 17:22 .ee
drwx------  2 sttp1553 sttp1553 4096 Jan 10 17:46 .elm
-rwxr-xr-x  1 sttp1553 sttp1553  333 Aug 30 20:04 .emacs
drwx------  3 sttp1553 sttp1553 4096 Jan 19 17:26 .enlightenment
drwxr-xr-x  6 sttp1553 sttp1553 4096 Jan 19 17:26 .gnome
drwxrwxr-x  2 sttp1553 sttp1553 4096 Dec 12 17:15 .gnome-desktop
drwxr-xr-x  2 sttp1553 sttp1553 4096 Sep  1 15:55 .gnome-help-browser
drwx------  2 sttp1553 sttp1553 4096 Aug 31 15:09 .gnome_private
drwxrwxr-x  2 sttp1553 sttp1553 4096 Oct 26 17:31 .gnp
drwxr-xr-x  3 sttp1553 sttp1553 4096 Aug 30 20:04 .kde
-rw-r--r--  1 sttp1553 sttp1553  665 Dec  5 17:03 .kderc
drwxrwxr-x  2 sttp1553 sttp1553 4096 Jan 18 17:19 .mc
drwxrwxr-x  5 sttp1553 sttp1553 4096 Dec  5 16:26 .netscape
-rw-rw-r--  1 sttp1553 sttp1553 13738 Jan 10 16:17 .pinerc
-rw-r--r--  1 sttp1553 sttp1553 3394 Aug 30 20:04 .screenrc
drwx------  3 sttp1553 sttp1553 4096 Aug 31 15:13 .xauth
-rw-------  1 sttp1553 sttp1553  253 Jan 19 17:26 .xsession-errors
drwxr-xr-x  5 sttp1553 sttp1553 4096 Aug 30 20:04 Desktop
```

The following is from a SuSe system.

```
rw-r--r--  1 sttp1553 users 6869 Jan 20 13:04 .X.err
-rw-r--r-- 1 sttp1553 users 5742 Jul 30 15:44 .Xdefaults
-rw-r--r-- 1 sttp1553 users 1305 Jul 30 15:44 .Xmodmap
lrwxrwxrwx 1 root     root    10 Jul 30 15:44 .Xresources ->>
                                              .Xdefaults
-rw-r--r-- 1 sttp1553 users    0 Jan 13 15:58 .addressbook
-rw------- 1 sttp1553 users 2285 Jan 13 15:58 .addressbook.lu
-rw------- 1 sttp1553 users 6214 Jan 20 12:12 .bash_history
-rw-r--r-- 1 sttp1553 users 1392 Jul 30 15:44 .bashrc
-rw-r--r-- 1 sttp1553 users    0 Jul 30 15:44 .dayplan
-rw------- 1 sttp1553 users    0 Jul 30 15:44 .dayplan.priv
-rw-r--r-- 1 sttp1553 users  208 Jul 30 15:44 .dvipsrc
-rw-r--r-- 1 sttp1553 users 4143 Jul 30 15:44 .emacs
-rw-r--r-- 1 sttp1553 users 1124 Jul 30 15:44 .exrc
-rw-r--r-- 1 sttp1553 users 5376 Jul 30 15:44 .gimprc
```

```
drwx------ 2 sttp1553 users   4096 Jul 30 15:44 .grok
-rw------- 1 sttp1553 users     18 Dec 20 12:31 .history
drwxr-xr-x 2 sttp1553 users   4096 Jul 30 15:44 .hotjava
-rw-r—r— 1 sttp1553 users   7924 Jul 30 15:44 .jazz
drwx------ 3 sttp1553 users   4096 Jul 30 15:59 .kde
-rw-r—r— 1 sttp1553 users    308 Jan 20 13:04 .kderc
-rw-r—r— 1 sttp1553 users    164 Jul 30 15:44 .kermrc
-rw-r—r— 1 sttp1553 users      0 Dec  8 17:13 .kmid_collections
-rw-r—r— 1 sttp1553 users      5 Nov 27 00:01 .kss-install.pid.suse
-rw-r—r— 1 sttp1553 users  10376 Jul 30 15:44 .lyxrc
-rw-r—r— 1 sttp1553 users   2286 Jul 30 15:44 .muttrc
-rw-r—r— 1 sttp1553 users   2070 Jul 30 15:44 .nc_keys
drwx------ 5 sttp1553 users   4096 Jan 20 12:58 .netscape
-rw------- 1 sttp1553 users      0 Dec  8 16:03 .newsrc-news
-rw------- 1 sttp1553 users     63 Dec  8 16:08 .newsrc-news.kcl.ac.uk
-rw-r—r— 1 sttp1553 users  13738 Jan  4 14:17 .pinerc
-rw------- 1 sttp1553 users     93 Dec 19 14:01 .plumberscores
-rw-r—r— 1 sttp1553 users    492 Jul 30 15:44 .profile
-rw-r—r— 1 sttp1553 users     54 Aug 30 08:35 .saves-653-suse.home~
-rw-r—r— 1 sttp1553 users     52 Oct  9 12:57 .saves-709-suse.home~
drwx------ 2 sttp1553 users   4096 Jul 30 15:44 .seyon
drwxr-xr-x 2 sttp1553 users   4096 Jul 30 15:59 .skel
-rw-r—r— 1 sttp1553 users     42 Jul 30 15:44 .stonxrc
-rw-r—r— 1 sttp1553 users     94 Jul 30 15:44 .susephone
-rw-r—r— 1 sttp1553 users      8 Jul 30 15:44 .tex
-rw-r—r— 1 sttp1553 users  10972 Jul 30 15:44 .uitrc.console
-rw-r—r— 1 sttp1553 users   9394 Jul 30 15:44 .uitrc.vt100
-rw-r—r— 1 sttp1553 users   9394 Jul 30 15:44 .uitrc.vt102
-rw-r—r— 1 sttp1553 users  10687 Jul 30 15:44 .uitrc.xterm
-rw-r—r— 1 sttp1553 users    324 Jul 30 15:44 .urlview
-rw-r—r— 1 sttp1553 users    341 Jul 30 15:44 .vimrc
-rw-r—r— 1 sttp1553 users   7913 Jul 30 15:44 .xcoralrc
drwxr-xr-x 2 sttp1553 users   4096 Jul 30 15:44 .xfm
-rwxr-xr-x 1 sttp1553 users   2036 Jul 30 15:44 .xinitrc
-rw-r—r— 1 sttp1553 users    795 Jul 30 15:44 .xserverrc.secure
-rwxr-xr-x 1 sttp1553 users   2751 Jul 30 15:44 .xsession
-rw-r—r— 1 sttp1553 users    119 Jul 30 15:44 .xtalkrc
-rw-r—r— 1 sttp1553 users     10 Jul 30 15:44 .zsh
```

As you can see there are similarities and differences. You have to get familiar with the files related to your Linux version.

Have a look in the

- .netscape

directory. You will see a lot of files and subdirectories that are created by Netscape when it runs. It is necessary to clear up the files periodically. Do a

- cd .netscape

then type

- du -k

to see how much file space is taken up by these files.

Environment variables

The following is the output from

- set

under SuSe linux.

```
BASH=/bin/bash
BASH_VERSINFO=([0]="2" [1]="03" [2]="0" [3]="1" [4]="release"
[5]="i386-suse-linux")
BASH_VERSION='2.03.0(1)-release'
COLORTERM=1
COLUMNS=80
DIRSTACK=()
DISPLAY=:0
EUID=500
GNOMEDIR=/opt/gnome
GROUPS=()
HISTCONTROL=ignoredups
HISTFILE=/home/sttp1553/.bash_history
HISTFILESIZE=500
HISTSIZE=500
HOME=/home/sttp1553
HOSTNAME=suse
HOSTTYPE=i386
IFS='
'
INFODIR=/usr/local/info:/usr/share/info:/usr/info
INFOPATH=/usr/local/info:/usr/share/info:/usr/info
KDEDIR=/opt/kde
LANG=POSIX
LC_COLLATE=POSIX
LD_LIBRARY_PATH=/opt/kde/lib
```

```
LESS='-M -S -I'
LESSCHARSET=latin1
LESSKEY=/etc/lesskey.bin
LESSOPEN='|lesspipe.sh %s'
LINES=22
LM_LICENSE_FILE=/usr/local/flexlm/licenses/NAG.demo
LOGNAME=sttp1553
LS_COLORS='no=00:fi=00:di=01;34:ln=01:pi=40;33:so=01;35:bd=4
0;33;01:cd=40;33;01:ex=01;31:*.cmd=01;32:*.exe=01;32:*.com=0
1;32:*.btm=01;32:*.bat=01;32:*.tar=00;31:*.tgz=00;31:*.rpm=0
0;31:*.arj=00;31:*.taz=00;31:*.lzh=00;31:*.zip=00;31:*.z=00;
31:*.Z=00;31:*.gz=00;31:*.bz2=00;31:*.jpg=01;35:*.gif=01;35:
*.bmp=01;35:*.xbm=01;35:*.xpm=01;35:*.tif=01;35:*.png=01;35:
'
LS_OPTIONS='-N —color=tty -T 0'
MACHINE=i586
MACHTYPE=i386-suse-linux
MAIL=/var/spool/mail/sttp1553
MAILCHECK=60
MANPATH=/usr/local/man:/usr/share/man:/usr/man:/usr/X11R6/ma
n:/usr/openwin/man
MINICOM='-c on'
NNTPSERVER=news
OLDPWD=/home/sttp1553/f95
OPTERR=1
OPTIND=1
OSTYPE=linux
PAGER=less
PATH=/usr/local/bin:/usr/bin:/usr/X11R6/bin:/bin:/usr/games/
bin:/usr/games:/opt/gnome/bin:/opt/kde/bin:.
PIPESTATUS=([0]="0")
POVRAYOPT=-l/usr/lib/povray/include
PPID=673
PRINTER=lp
PROFILEREAD=true
PS1='\u@\h:\w >> '
PS2='>> '
PS4='+ '
PWD=/home/sttp1553
QTDIR=/usr/lib/qt
SHELL=/bin/bash
SHELLOPTS=braceexpand:hashall:histexpand:monitor:
privileged:ignoreeof:interactive-comments:emacs
SHLVL=4
SUSE_DOC_HOST=localhost
TERM=xterm
```

```
TEXINPUTS=':::~/.TeX:/usr/doc/.TeX:~/.TeX:/usr/doc/.TeX'
UID=500
USER=sttp1553
WINDOWMANAGER=/usr/X11R6/bin/kde
XKEYSYMDB=/usr/X11R6/lib/X11/XKeysymDB
XNLSPATH=/usr/X11R6/lib/X11/nls
_=..
ignoreeof=0
no_proxy=localhost
s=/etc/profile.d/tetex.sh
remount=()
{
    /bin/mount -o remount,$*
}
startx=()
{
    /usr/X11R6/bin/startx $* 2>>&1 | tee ~/.X.err
}
```

At login the Bourne shell reads the initialization files /etc/profile and $HOME/.profile. You cannot change the content of /etc/profile, but you have permission to edit the contents of .profile, which is in your home directory and is owned by you.

Making permanent settings

To set an environment variable and make it permanent, edit the .profile file and add the settings you want. The following is a .profile file from a SuSe system. The last two lines are the ones of interest. These are required by the NAG Fortran 95 compiler.

```
# .profile is read for all login shells
# all other interactive shells will read .bashrc
# So read .bashrc also from .profile and make all changes
  to bashrc.
# Then you should always have your correct setup.

test -z "$PROFILEREAD" && . /etc/profile

if test -f ~/.bashrc; then
```

```
  . ~/.bashrc
fi
#
# some people don't like fortune.  If you have humor,
# please enable it by
# uncommenting the following lines.
#
#if [ -x /usr/bin/fortune ] ; then
#   echo
#   /usr/bin/fortune
#   echo
#fi
LM_LICENSE_FILE=/usr/local/flexlm/licenses/NAG.demo
export LM_LICENSE_FILE
```

Summary

It is only possible to give brief coverage of what can be done with Unix and Linux in this chapter. Further material is given in the bibliography.

Bibliography

Deitel, H.M., *An Introduction to Operating Systems*, Addison Wesley

- This is a very good introduction to operating systems. There is coverage of several actual operating systems in the case study section.

Robbins, A., *Unix in a Nutshell*, O'Reilly.

- Terse but comprehensive summary of Unix. If you had to buy one Unix book then this is probably it.

Seiver, E., *Linux in a Nutshell*, O'Reilly

- Similar to the above but this targets Linux specifically.

Rosenblatt, B., *Learning the Korn Shell*, O'Reilly.

- Korn shell coverage.

DuBois, P., *Using csh and tcsh*, O'Reilly.

- csh and tcsh coverage.

MKS, *MKS Toolkit User Guide*, Mortice Kern Systems Inc.

- This is one of the books that come with the MKS Toolkit that provides Unix functionality under DOS and Windows. The first version I have came on 5 1/4 inch 360 Kb floppy disks! Quite a good coverage of the Korn shell and their own Windows Korn shell. You can create simple Windows-style interaction with a user with this shell.

Bourne, S. R., *The Unix System*, Addison Wesley.

- This is one of the first Unix books I ever bought. Written by the person working at Bell Labs who wrote the Bourne shell.

Chivers, I.D. & Sleightholme, J., *Introducing Fortran 95*, Springer Verlag.

- This is the book that has the Fortran 95 examples that are used in the pattern matching example in this chapter.

Chapter

10

Installing Software

The aim of this chapter is to look briefly at installing software.

Software can be installed in a variety of ways:

- raw Unix
- package managers
- package managers with a graphical or windows interface.

We will look at actual examples of all three in this chapter. The availability of relatively easy to use graphical packages for software installation is one of the reasons behind the increasing use of Linux.

RPM

RPM stands for Red Hat Package Manager and is distributable under the terms of the GPL. It is installed with Red Hat Linux and SuSe Linux. Type

- man rpm

to see what options are available.

What is installed?

The command

- rpm -q -a > rpm_list.txt

will provide a list of each of the installed packages. I recommend redirecting the output to a file. I also recommend sorting the file. This can be done by typing

- sort < rpm_list.txt > sorted_rpm_list.txt

and is much easier to work with. You then have a record of what was installed on your system at that time. I printed it after sorting to have a permanent record in the event of a system crash.

Gnome RPM – GnoRPM

Gnome RPM was introduced in Red Hat Linux 6.0 and is a graphical RPM tool. It can be accessed in a variety of ways on a Red Hat system. It is not installed under SuSe Linux.

The following is a screenshot of GnoRPM from a Red Hat 6.2 system.

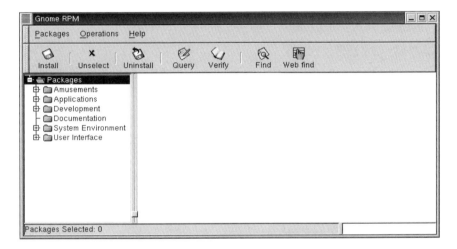

The following screenshot shows what languages are installed.

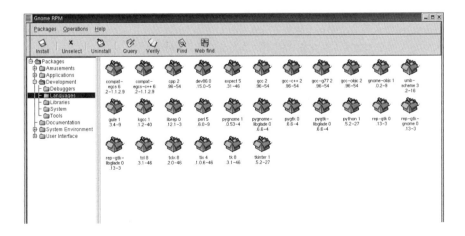

YaST

SuSe Linux has a couple of tools to help here. One can be invoked from a simple terminal window, the other requires an X-Windows session. Both offer similar functionality. The key thing is that there will be an option from the menu system to manipulate packages. We will look at example of using one of these later in this chapter.

Compression

Software is often distributed in a compressed format. This is to save time when downloading and to enable more software to be included on a CD, for example. We will look into this briefly, as in some of what follows you will need to know something about compression to complete the software installation successfully.

gzip and gunzip

gzip (GNU zip) is a compression utility designed to be a replacement for compress. Its main advantages over compress are much better compression and freedom from patented algorithms. gzip was developed as a replacement for compress because of the UNISYS and IBM patents covering the LZW algorithm used by compress.

It has been adopted by the GNU project. Their home page is:

- http://www.gzip.org/

Files with names ending with .gz are created by

- gzip

and files with names ending in .gz, .z, .Z, .tgz, .taz can be read by its partner

- gunzip.

gzip

To compress a single file, type

- gzip <filename>

which compresses the file, adding .gz to the filename.

To compress each file in a directory and all of its subdirectories type

- gzip -r <directory_name>

gunzip

- gunzip <filename>

decompresses a single file.

- gunzip -r <directory_name>

decompresses all compressed files in a directory and its subdirectories.

Refer to the man or info pages for more information.

Multiple files

To manage multiple files it is common to use the tar utility.

- tar -cvf tarfile.tar files

will create a tar file.

- tar -xvf tarfile

will extract the files.

Refer to the info or man pages for more information.

Mounting the CD-Rom drive

The first thing to do if installing from a CD is to mount the drive. Inserting the CD should be enough if automounting is supported.

If not, the following command is an example taken from a SuSe Linux system:

- mount -t -iso9660 /dev/cdrom /mnt/cdrom

Only root can do this by default.

The following command

- ls -la /mnt/cdrom

will show the contents of the CD.

The following command will provide details of the mounted file systems:

- df -k

including the CD.

The following command will unmount the CD:

- umount /mnt/cdrom

The CD can also be accessed from the desktop of course.

Adobe Acrobat

An increasing amount of documentation is being made available in what is called Adobe Acrobat Portable Document Format (PDF). Acrobat readers are freely available both from Adobe's website and on CDs available with computer magazines. It may be installed with later Linux distributions. Adobe's home site is:

- http://www.adobe.com/

Follow the links. You will need to provide a small number of personal details. It is too big to download over a telephone line! At the time of the download the file was called

- linux-ar-405.tar.gz

Follow the instructions provided.

The installation will fail under SuSe Linux as they do not make

- ed

available by default.

SuSe 6.4 Linux and ed

For some reason SuSe Linux does not install ed by default with the 'standard' install. Log in and type

- su

to switch to root.

Then type

- startx

to bring up the windows environment.

The panel at the bottom should have one button labelled YaST. Click on this. If you aren't root it will prompt for the root password. You will see a screen similar to the following:

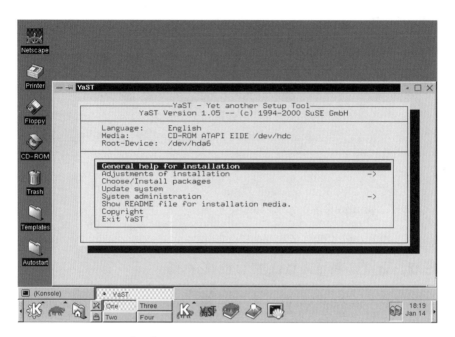

Insert the first SuSe 6.4 CD. Then select

- Choose/Install packages

This will bring the following screen:

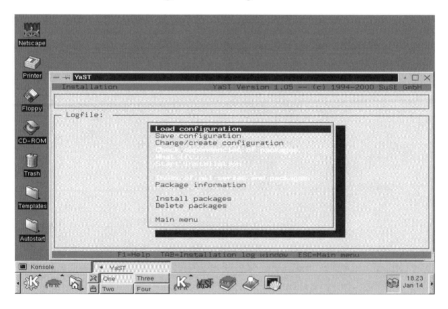

Next select

● Load configuration

This will bring up a screen similar to the following:

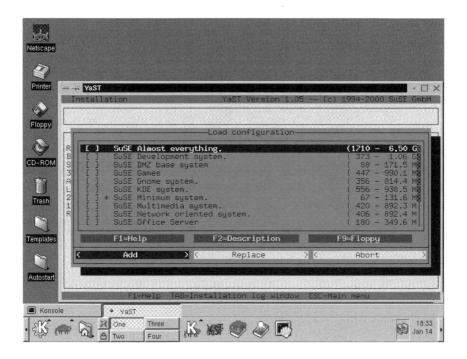

Scroll down to your most up to date installation. This is taken from a SuSe 6 system.

In this example I've installed

● SuSe Default system

and added two more:

● base and tetex and g77

and

● base and latex.

I choose the last. This then returns you to the earlier screen.

Next select

● Package information.

This brings up a screen like:

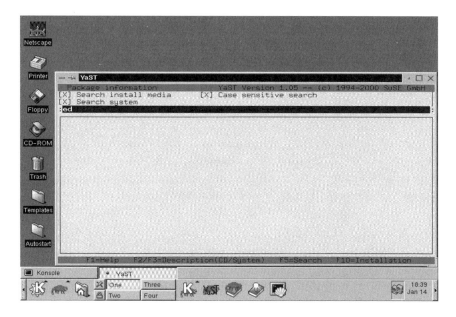

I've already typed the name of the package I'm interested in
– ed. F5 will then start the search. You'll then be presented
with a screen similar to the following and you can scroll
round until you've found the one you want.

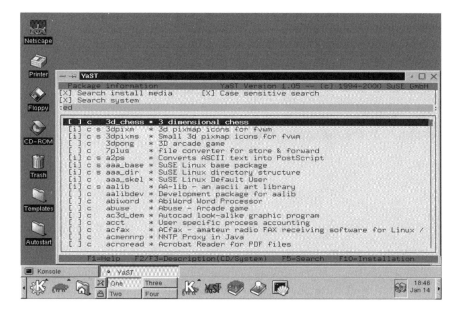

The left-hand column has

- [ ]

or

- [i]

to indicate what is installed. Locate ed and press the space bar and this will bring up an X in the check box. F10 starts the installation. You will eventually be presented with a screen with a <Continue> option highlighted. Press the [return] key and the installation will start. ed is quite small so this won't take very long.

You will then be dropped back to the Load configuration screen. Now save the configuration. You have to provide a name and description.

Next choose save, and choose hard disk. This takes you back to the Load configuration screen. Choosing Main menu will start the SuSeConfig Tool which will update all necessary files.

Eventually this will complete and <Continue> will be highlighted at the bottom of the screen. Press return.

From the main menu choose

- Exit YaST.

That's it!

GNU Fortran 77

This is a free Fortran 77 compiler. It is a popular choice for numeric programming under Linux. A GNU Fortran 95 compiler is already in the pipeline.

Red Hat Linux

The compiler is installed by default.

SuSe 6.4 Linux

Follow the steps given for ed given earlier.

NAG Intel g77 Double Precision Numeric Library

This is a commercial product. NAG provide a high performance numeric library for the GNU Fortran 77 compiler – g77. The NAG home page is:

- http://www.nag.co.uk/

They distribute the library as a tar file. It can be installed by the following command:

- tar -xvf /mnt/cdrom/fl99.tar

assuming that you have mounted the CD Rom drive using

- mount -t iso9660 /dev/cdrom /mnt/cdrom

which works on both Red Hat and SuSe Linux.

Switch to super user and move to

- /usr/local

before issuing the tar command. This will then install according to the recommendations in the Filesystem Hierarchy Standard.

The library called libnag.a is copied into

- /usr/lib

The man pages are moved using

- mv nag_fl_un.3 /usr/local/man/man3

to make available the documentation.

There is a simple script called nagexample to compile and run the examples. This is copied over to

- /usr/local/bin

The following shell variables have to be set:

- nagfdir="fllux19dg"
- fcompile="g77"
- flink="-lnag".

These lines need to be uncommented out.

The default in Red Hat 6.2 and 7 is not to run executables in the default directory. You will need to alter the .bash_profile file to allow execution of the nagexample file from wherever you are in the directory hierarchy.

I work with two versions of the library for Linux. The other version is for NAG's own Fortran 95 compiler. This is available from NAG for a 30-day evaluation.

If you want a fully featured Fortran 95 compiler then this is one to consider. You might like to visit the Polyhedron home site for a Windows and Linux Fortran compiler comparison. Their home address is:

- http://www.polyhedron.co.uk/

Java

Sun have made versions of Java freely available on their web-sites. It is necessary to install at least the Java SDK and documentation if you are going to program with Java. If you have a reasonably powerful system I would also recommend installing the development environment.

There are a number of useful Web addresses. Try

- http://www.java.sun.com/
- http://www.java.sun.com/j2se/1.3/download-linux.html

This page offered the options of downloading

- the development environment
- the jdk
- the documentation.

I recommend getting all three.

Who knows what will be working when you try getting the software!

Java SDK

This was available as:

- Red Hat RPM shell script
- GNUZIP Tar shell script.

Choose whichever you want. There are clear instructions given in the installation notes.

Java development environment

This is called Fotre for Java. It is a quite well-featured IDE. Follow the installation instructions.

Java documentation

English and Japanese versions are available and there is also a search engine. Follow the installation instructions.

Summary

We have covered several ways of doing software installations in this chapter.

Bibliography

The Linux platform is quite well served with compilers, especially for scientific and Web programming. There are also a number of libraries available. Two very well regarded commercial numeric libraries are provided by NAG and Visual Numerics. Their Web addresses are:

- http://www.nag.co.uk/
- http://www.vni.com/

You should also have a look at Netlib. Their home page is

- http://www.netlib.org/

The software is free but you use it at your own risk. No support is offered and their motto is *Anything free comes with no guarantee!*

Chapter 11

Text Formatting and Document Production

The chapter looks at some of the tools available under Linux for text formatting and document production. There is coverage of both conventional paper document production and electronic document production. A document could be

- a letter
- coursework
- a report
- a research paper
- a dissertation
- a manual
- Web pages

and can be a combination of text and graphical material. Unix has been used for document production since its very beginning at Bell Labs in the 1970s. The paper by Kernighan et al is dated 1978 and provides a good background to using a general purpose system for document production.

We are seeing an increasing use of the Web as a mechanism for information dissemination and being able to use a program or package to target both printed and Web copies is obviously very useful.

Electronic publishing basics

Most people have used a word processor for producing documents and may find the idea of splitting a document into two parts a little strange. These are the text and the mark-up that defines how things will get laid out. More experienced users will probably have got used to using so-called style sheets which help get a consistent look and feel to a document.

The first systems at Bell Labs had the following programs for document production

- NRoff – Run Off, targeting simple output devices
- Troff – Typesetter Roff, targeting high quality typesetting devices
- Tbl   – Table generating program
- Eqn   – Equation setting program

and they were ported to a number of non-Unix platforms. Whilst not widely used today they did pave the way for the acceptance of Unix as a platform for document production, and in thinking about document production as a set of steps:

- text preparation using an editor
- running a program with the text as input
- the program generating an output file (sometimes in a so-called device-independent format) that would be post-processed for display on the screen or printer

which has proved a very effective way of working when involved on a regular basis with document production.

This compares with so-called What You See Is What You Get with a word processing package like Microsoft Word.

Some high-end systems combine the best of both of these ways of working, e.g.

- Quark Express
- Framemaker
- Corel Ventura Publisher.

These are used extensively by professionals, where the steep learning curve pays off with the ease of production of complex documents.

Text tools

Unix provides a range of commands that make the task of manipulating text files easier. These include

- cat   – display the contents of a file
- wc   – word count
- head   – the first part of a file
- tail   – the last part of a file
- last   – some people find this easier to use than head or tail
- awk   – process a file using a script
- sed   – process a file using a script
- perl   – process a file using a script

- vi   – powerful pattern matching editor
- emacs – powerful pattern matching editor
- comm – compare two files on a line by line basis
- diff   – similar to the above
- csplit   – split a file into chunks
- cut   – select a list of columns or fields from one or more files
- fold   – break lines so that they are not wider than a specified width
- grep   – search a file for a string
- join   – join two files on common columns
- paste   – merge files according to common values
- sort   – powerful sorting tool
- spell   – spelling checker
- split   – split a file into line segments
- uniq   – remove duplicate lines from a sorted file.

These can be used in conjunction with the text processing tools. The key concept is that of several small sharp tools being used in conjunction to achieve a complex task. Another key idea is that of automating the process so that if something changes the process can be run again automatically to achieve the desired effect, rather than using a program with a graphical interface, where there is no real record of the sequence of what was done and no ability to replay it. Note that this is not a criticism of software with a graphical interface. One of the reasons for the success of Windows and Linux is the easy to use graphical software that exists. Rather it is the way that commands and programming complement this and together make you much more productive.

TeX

TeX is the work of Donald Knuth who is a professor at Stanford University. He was supported by the National Science Foundation, the Office of Naval Research, the IBM Corporation, and had the backing of the American Mathematical Society during the 10 years or so that he did the original development work. TeX was designed as a computer type-setting system for the production of high quality mathematics. Whilst this is its forte it has since been used for all kinds of document production. TeX is installed on most Linux systems.

I first came across TeX over 20 years ago at Imperial College. User documentation was required as part of the computer service and if this was text then things were relatively straightforward. Enter mathematics. In the typesetting environment of the time mathematics was classified as penalty copy. TeX changed this. It is now possible to typeset equations with relative ease with TeX and its add-ons.

LaTeX

LaTeX is extension to TeX that many people find easier to use. It is essentially a collection of commands that allow people to concentrate on document structure. If you've used Word you may have used a so-called style sheet where the style sheet ensured a consistent look and feel for a document in terms of headings, normally justified paragraphs, indented sections, headers and footers, etc. LaTeX is often installed on Linux and Unix systems.

The original version of LaTeX was conceived by Leslie Lamport as a set of additional macros for TeX. LatEx2e is probably to be found on your Linux distribution.

Fonts

It is becoming more necessary to be able to work with information exchanged electronically written in a wide variety of languages, and people expect the information to display correctly. This requires that fonts are available for each of these languages at least. To see what come installed on a Windows system, have a look within the Control Panel at the Fonts icon. Most of these will be commercial fonts. Someone has paid for them.

In the Linux world many people are prepared to put fonts into the public domain. See the Fonts FAQ for more details.

W3C

The World Wide Web Consortium (W3C) is involved in developing technologies (and this can be a specification, guidelines, software or tools) to help the Web evolve as a platform for information, commerce and communication. Their home page is:

- http://www.w3.org/

Graphics formats

There is a range of graphics formats used and they fall into two broad camps – vector and bitmap. Simplistically a bitmap is a two-dimensional array of points that may have colour information associated with each point. Hence a circle on your screen may involve many thousands of bytes of information. The same circle described in a vector format would be very small as it could be described in terms of a centre and a radius. Both have their strengths and weaknesses.

Bitmap

The following are some commonly used bitmap formats:

- GIF
- TIFF
- BMP
- JPEG
- PNG.

There are a number of packages that will work with images in these formats including:

- Electric Eyes – Red Hat Linux
- Image Viewer – SuSe Linux.

They are widely used.

Portable Network Graphics (PNG)

PNG is a W3C extensible file format for the loss-free, portable, well compressed storage of raster images. PNG provides a patent-free replacement for GIF and can also replace many common uses of TIFF. Indexed-colour, greyscale, and true colour images are supported, plus an optional alpha channel for transparency. Sample depths range from 1 to 16 bits.

Vector graphics

For an introduction to this area have a look at the Foley and van Dam book.

SVG is a W3C language for describing two-dimensional graphics in XML. SVG allows for three types of graphic objects: vector graphic shapes (e.g. paths consisting of straight lines and curves), images and text. Graphical objects can be grouped, styled, transformed and composed into previously rendered objects. Their home site is:

- http://www.w3.org/Graphics/SVG/Overview.htm8

HTML

HTML is the mark-up language of the Web. It stands for HyperText Markup Language, and it allows the user to format text, add rules, graphics, sound, video and save it all in text-only ASCII files that any computer can read.

Visit the W3C website for more information:

- http://www.w3.org/MarkUp/

Portable Document Format (PDF)

PDF has become the native file format of the Adobe Acrobat family of products, and enables people to exchange and view electronic documents easily and reliably, independently of the environment in which they were created. PDF builds on the PostScript page description language, layering a document structure and interactive navigation features on PostScript's underlying imaging model.

It has succeeded because Adobe give away Acrobat readers, and this is a very common Internet browser helper. As you have seen, much of the documentation that comes with Linux is in PDF format.

PostScript

PostScript is a programming language that describes the appearance of text, sampled images and graphics on a printed page or display. PostScript language interpreters have been incorporated into many printers, typesetters, film records, and computer display environments.

Ghostscript

Ghostscript will be found on most Unix and Linux systems and can be used to display both PDF and PostScript files.

XML

XML stands for Extensible Markup Language, and is intended to be a platform-independent language for describing data. It is rapidly establishing itself as a way of solving a range of information and data interchange problems – increasingly important in a networked world. For more information visit:

- http://www.w3.org/XML/

Summary

The intentions of this chapter were to make you aware of some of the tools that exist under Linux for text formatting and document production, including publishing to the Web. Tools exists for:

- LaTeX to HTML
- LaTeX to PDF

to name just two. This means that it is relatively straightforward to publish to a variety of Web formats and paper, from one source file. Tools also exist to massage text files in an enormous number of ways. The tool set is extensible. A number of sources of further information have been provided.

This is another reason for the take-up of Linux.

Bibliography

Kernighan, B.W., Lesk, M.E., Ossanna, J.F. Jr., *Document Production*, The Bell System Technical Journal, Vol 57, No. 6, July–August 1978.

- The paper provides a good look at how Unix has been used for document production. There is brief coverage of Troff, Nroff, Eqn, Tbl and macros.

Knuth, D., The *TeXbook*, Addison Wesley.

- The original TeX book. Most people aren't prepared to devote the time and effort to use what I would call raw TeX and so never consider reading this book. A pity as Knuth writes very well.

Clark, M., *A Plain TeX Primer*, OUP.
- Malcolm and I worked together at Imperial College. He stumbled into the world of TeX at Imperial College by agreeing to typeset information on chlorine for the International Union of Pure and Applied Chemistry. He did it with a TeX implementation that was in a beta development stage. This is not recommended. The rest is history.

Lamport, L., LateX, *A Document Production System*, Addison Wesley.

- The original LaTeX book. A gentle introduction.

Goossens, M., Mittelbach, F., Samarin, A., *The LaTeX Companion*, Addison Wesley.

- Probably your second LaTeX book.

Goossens, M., *The LaTeX Graphics Companion*, Addison Wesley

- Your third LaTeX book.

Foley, J.D., van Dam, A., Feiner, S.K. & Hughes, J.F., *Computer Graphics, Principles and Practice*, Addison Wesley,

- The best book I've found on graphics. Highly recommended.

The W3C home site.

- http://www.w3.org/

The home page for the Fonts FAQ

- http://www.linux.org/docs/ldp/howto/Font-HOWTO.html

Chapter 12

Programming Languages

The chapter looks at programming languages under Linux. The emphasis is on scientific or numeric programming.

There are a lot of programming languages available for Linux. In this chapter we will look at some of them. The emphasis is on languages used in numeric and scientific computing.

History

The Fortran language goes back to the 1950s and was originally developed by a team working for IBM under John Backus. It was designed as a language for FORmula TRANslation – i.e. numeric computation. It has been standardized several times giving rise to Fortran 66, Fortran 77, Fortran 90, Fortran 95; Fortran 2000 is the next version. Its forte is numeric computation but with the Fortran 90 standard it became a very powerful and expressive modern programming language, whilst still retaining its strength in the numeric area. If you want an accurate weather forecast today then this will be done using Fortran. High-performance computing is dominated by Fortran and at a recent BCS meeting it was stated that 90% of the work run on the Cray supercomputer at Manchester was Fortran based. This machine is one of the most powerful in the UK and is in the world's top 20.

C was developed by Kernighan and Ritchie at Bell Labs. Bell Labs was the research laboratory of the Bell Telephone Company in the US. It was designed as a systems implementation language and was used to rewrite some 95% of the Unix operating system. Only 5% or so ended up being written in assembler. The Unix tools are written in C and are a very good example of what C is best at: the construction of sharp, small tools. The first (unofficial standard) was the original Kernighan and Ritchie book in 1978. The first official standard was 1989. Its successor is already in the pipeline. Have a look at

- http://www.c9x.org/

for up to date information regarding the state of the latest version.

C++ was an attempt by Bjarne Stroustrup to produce an object-oriented version of C. He had been exposed to Simula early on and realized the benefits of a language like that. Simula is a product of the 1960s. The first version of Simula was available in 1967. Object-oriented programming is not new! Simula was widely used for discrete event simulation. C++ was finally standardized in 1997. The last couple of years have seen the emergence of some good standard conformant compilers and a number of well-written books.

Sun are the company responsible for the development of Java. Java is evolving. There were (as of December 2000) four major versions around, and these are 1.0.x, 1.1.x, 1.2.x. and 1.3.x.

- 1.0.x – The first release was in early 1996. 1.0.2 was the version used in the first college course offered at King's.
- 1.1.x – Early 1997. Added a new event-handling mechanism. By now the primitive nature of the AWT (Abstract Windows Toolkit) had become apparent. 1997 saw the introduction of the Java Foundation Classes that superseded and included AWT. These new components were called Swing. JavaBeans came into existence. JavaBeans is a component architecture for the Java platform.
- 1.2.x aka Java 2 – Sun re-badged Java in December 1998 when Java 1.2 became Java 2.
- 1.3.x

Other companies have also shown an interest, including IBM and Microsoft. There is no official Java standard at this time and it is not clear if there will be in the near future due to Sun's withdrawal from the standardization effort.

We will also look at Perl. Other compilers are available and include Ada and Python.

C

The main C compiler for Linux is the GNU C compiler. The GNU project was launched in 1984 to develop a complete Unix-like operating system which is free. GNU stands for GNU's Not Unix and is pronounced guh-NEW. Their home address is

- http://www.gnu.org/

The Free Software Foundation (FSF) is a tax-exempt charity that raises funds for work on the GNU Project. Visit

- http://www.gnu.org/fsf/fsf.html

for more information about the FSF.

GCC is a free compiler collection for C, C++, Fortran, Objective C and other languages. It is installed with all of the Red Hat distributions mentioned in this book.

The compiler is invoked by typing

- gcc filename.c

and this will generate a file called

- a.out

that is the executable.

C++

The main C++ compiler for Linux is the GNU g++ compiler. It is normally bundled with their C compiler, gcc, and, therefore, is installed with the Red Hat distributions.

The compiler is invoked by typing

- g++ filename.cxx

and this will generate a file called

- a.out

that is the executable. The C++ teaching I'm involved with uses both the Sun C++ compiler and the GNU compiler. As the language was only standardized relatively recently there is a lot to learn from compiling with two or more compilers.

Intel/Linux Fortran compilers

There are a number of Fortran compilers for Linux. These include

- APF or Absoft Pro Fortran
- G77 or GNU Fortran 77
- LF95 or Lahey/Fujitsu LF95 Linux Express
- NAG or NAGWare f95
- NAS or N.A.Software FortranPlus.

A comparison of these compilers can be found at the Polyhedron website. Their home page is:

- http://www.polyhedron.co.uk/

Some factors to consider include

- price
- standard conformance
- language extensions
- diagnostic capabilities
- third party support – what libraries and other packages can you use?
- performance.

Your choice will depend on one or more of the above.

Fortran 77

GNU Fortran, or g77, is designed initially as a free replacement for the Unix f77 command. g77 consists of several components:

- A modified version of the gcc command.
- The g77 command itself, which also might be installed as the system's f77 command.

- The libg2c run-time library. This library contains the machine code needed to support capabilities of the Fortran language that are not directly provided by the machine code generated by the g77 compilation phase. libg2c is just the unique name g77 gives to its version of libf2c to distinguish it from any copy of libf2c installed from f2c.
- The compiler itself, internally named f771.

The g77 command is essentially just a front end for the gcc command. Fortran users will normally use g77 because g77 knows how to specify the libraries needed to link with Fortran programs (libg2c and lm).

The libf2c library is distributed with GNU Fortran. It contains the procedures needed by Fortran programs while they are running, e.g. while code generated by g77 is likely to do additions, subtractions, and multiplications in line, in the actual compiled code it is not likely to do trigonometric functions this way. Instead, operations like trigonometric functions are compiled by the f771 compiler into machine code that, when run, calls on functions in libg2c, so libg2c must be linked with almost every useful program having any component compiled by GNU Fortran. The g77 command takes care of all this for you.

Fortran 90

The Fortran 90 standard has been overtaken by the Fortran 95 standard. If possible you should only consider Fortran 95 conformant compilers.

Fortran 95

There are a number of Fortran 95 conformant compilers. We will only look at one of them here, the NAG f95 compiler.

NAG f95

A 30-day evaluation version is available from NAG. NAG produced the world's first Fortran 90 compiler and it has been in use at King's under the Solaris operating system since the replacement of our central DEC/Compaq systems with Sun systems.

It is available on a CD and we look at the installation and use of this compiler. It generates C code at the back end and requires the installation of the GNU C compiler for the code generation stage. These should be installed with both SuSe and Red Hat Linux.

The following information was taken from the CD:

```
Machine: Intel Pentium (i586)
Operating System: Linux 2.0.27 (RedHat 4.1) and
Linux 2.2.5-15 (RedHat 6.0)
C Compiler: gcc 2.7.2.1 (RedHat 4.1) and egcs 2.91.66
(RedHat 6.0)
Space Required: 5.2 MB for RedHat 4.1, 5.9 MB for RedHat 6.0

64-bit integers: YES
Garbage Collection: YES
128-bit reals: NO
```

Separate executables and library files are provided for Red Hat 6.0 systems and earlier systems due to differences in the respective C libraries. The installation process detects which version of the C library is available and installs the appropriate files.

g95 project

The goal of the g95 project is to create a free, open-source Fortran 95 compiler. The code has been donated to the Free Software Foundation for inclusion in GCC, the GNU Compiler Collection. g95 is in an embryonic state. The current g95 does nothing except print the contents of internal data structures. Timescales are difficult to judge as to when a reasonable working version will become available.

Java

Java is available from Sun's site. Their home address is:

● http://www.java.sun.com/

The address for the Linux versions is

● http://www.java.sun.com/j2se/1.3/download-linux.html

This provides links to the Java 2 SDK, Standard Edition, Version 1.3.0.

Scroll down to download the JavaTM 2 SDK, Standard Edition and documentation. Sun recommend using an IDE and the supporting IDE for J2SETM Version 1.3 for Linux is called Forte for Java, Community Edition. You should also download the Java 2 SDK, v 1.3.0 documentation. This is essential. They also provide Java Technology on the Linux Platform, A Guide to Getting Started, for tips on developing on the Linux platform. There is a Red Hat RPM shell script for the install.

Practical extraction and report language (Perl)

Perl is a language for processing text files, extracting information from those text files, and printing reports based on that information. It was already installed under both SuSe and Red Hat Linux. Considerable documentation is provided and the following were some of the man pages under SuSe Linux 6.0

perlfaq	– Perl frequently asked questions
perltoc	– Perl documentation table of contents
perldata	– Perl data structures
perlsyn	– Perl syntax
perlop	– Perl operators and precedence
perlre	– Perl regular expressions

perlrun	– Perl execution and options
perlfunc	– Perl built-in functions
perlopentut	– Perl open() tutorial
perlvar	– Perl predefined variables
perlsub	– Perl subroutines
perlmod	– Perl modules: how they work
perlmodlib	– Perl modules: how to write and use
perlmodinstall	– Perl modules: how to install from CPAN
perlform	– Perl formats
perlref	– Perl references
perlreftut	– Perl references short introduction
perldsc	– Perl data structures intro
perllol	– Perl data structures: lists of lists
perltoot	– Perl OO tutorial
perlobj	– Perl objects
perltie	– Perl objects hidden behind simple variables
perlbot	– Perl OO tricks and examples
perlipc	– Perl inter-process communication
perlthrtut	– Perl threads tutorial
perlsec	– Perl security
perltrap	– Perl traps for the unwary
perlport	– Perl portability guide
perlstyle	– Perl style guide

If you require a paper book then several are available and the bibliography gives some details of a couple.

Perl has features taken from C, awk, sed and sh and if you have familiarity with one or more of these then you should be able to pick it up relatively quickly. Converters are also available to convert from the awk and sed into Perl:

- a2p – awk to perl translator
- s2p – sed to perl translator.

The Perl home site is

- http://www.perl.com/pub

Bibliography

Budd, T., *Data Structures in C++ Using the Standard Template Library*, Addison Wesley.

- Good introduction to the STL.

Chivers, I.D. & Sleightholme, J., *Introducing Fortran 95*, Springer Verlag.

- Gentle introduction to programming in Fortran 95.

Deitel, H.M. & Deitel, P.J., *C++ How to Program*, Prentice Hall.

- Good C++ text book.

Deitel, H.M. & Deitel, P.J., *Java How to Program*, Prentice Hall.

- Good Java text.

Kernighan, B.W. & Ritchie, D.M., *The C Programming Language*, 2nd Edition, Prentice Hall.

- The C book, written by the creators of the language.

Stroustrup, B., *The C++ Programming Language*, 3rd Edition, Addison Wesley.

- The C++ book written by the creator of the language.

Wall, L., Christiansen, T., & Schwartz, R., *Programming Perl*, O'Reilly.

- Definitive Perl book, not aimed at beginners.

Chapter

13

Miscellaneous

The aim of this chapter is to look at a number of other things that are not covered elsewhere.

Electronic mail – email

There are a number of issues to consider here including:

- access at home
- access at work
- mail clients – what program you use to read and manage your mail, also called mail user agents or mua
- mail servers – the program that actually sends and receives mail messages, also called mail transfer agents or mta.

We'll look at each in turn.

Email at home

This is probably going to be easiest via a Web interface. Netscape is installed under Linux and it is then just a question of connecting to the Internet via a modem, for example, and starting Netscape.

Email at work

At work your email system may well have a Web interface in which case you could just use Netscape as you did at home, or you could use one of the mail user agents that come with Linux. We will look at a number of these.

Mail

Mail is a very basic client program. Type mail at the shell and see for yourself. Typing ? at the prompt will bring up a brief coverage of some of the essential commands.

Pine

Pine stands for Program for Internet News and Email and was developed at the University of Washington. It has a very straightforward interface based round simple keystrokes.

Elm

Elm is another mailer. It has a simple user interface.

Kmail

X-Windows-based mailers exist. Kmail is available under the KDE and can therefore be found on both SuSE and Red Hat platforms.

Sendmail

Sendmail is probably the most widely used mail transport agent running under Linux. It was written by Eric Allman whilst first a student and then a member of staff at the University of California at Berkeley. It went through a number of incarnations before being formally released as sendmail with BSD 4.1c.

A number of other people and organizations got involved and eventually sendmail has evolved into release V8.8 at the time of writing this chapter. End users should not see sendmail at all.

Email and security

This is an important issue and you will need to check with your local technical people about running sendmail. At King's several of our Unix systems have been hacked and used to relay so-called spam. The official policy is to recommend the use of the central College mail system, and disable local sendmail. Maintaining one system is obviously a lot easier than trying to maintain a myriad of widely systems.

Linux as a platform for a Web server

Linux is a popular choice as a Web server. The installations of SuSe and Red Hat versions described in this book will provide fully functional Web servers. The following screenshots are of a SuSe 6 system. The first is the home page, and the second is the opening page of the Apache on-line documentation.

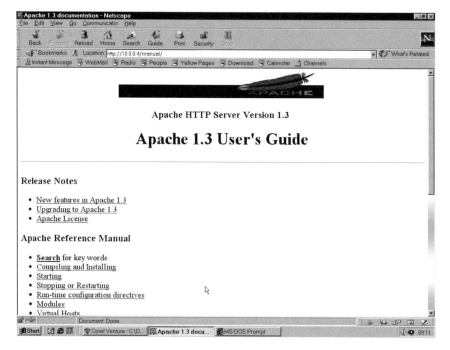

Apache was originally based on code and ideas found in the most popular HTTP server of the time – NCSA httpd 1.3 (early 1995). It has since evolved into a system which rivals most Unix-based HTTP servers in terms of functionality, efficiency and speed. Apache was, as of January 1997, the most popular WWW server on the Internet, according to a Netcraft Survey. As of June 1999 Apache ran on over 3 million Internet servers. Apache is "A PAtCHy server". It was based on some existing code and a series of "patch files".

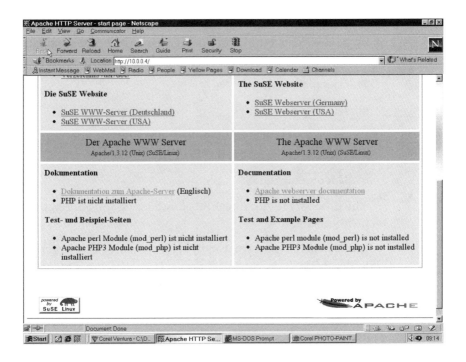

Apache

The Apache home page is

● http://www.apache.org/

The Apache Software Foundation (ASF) is a not-for-profit corporation, incorporated in Delaware, USA, in June of 1999. The ASF is a natural outgrowth of The Apache Group, a group of individuals that was initially formed in 1995 to develop the Apache HTTP Server.

The Apache Software Foundation exists to provide organizational, legal and financial support for the Apache open-source software projects. Formerly known as the Apache Group, the foundation has been set up as a membership-based, not-for-profit corporation, in order to ensure that the Apache projects continue to exist beyond the participation of individual volunteers, enable contributions of intellectual property and funds on a sound basis, and provide a vehicle for limiting legal exposure while participating in open-source software projects.

The key files are in the

- /etc/httpd

directory, and you should look at httpd.conf if you want to make changes. Probably the most important entry is

- DocumentRoot

which was set to /usr/local/httpd/htdocs on the SuSe system mentioned above.

If you switch to root you can then create a directory structure under this to hold your Web pages. The following screenshot illustrates a photograph of the London Eye in the

- photo

directory. Note the URL used in Netscape.

Database management

Linux is a good platform for database management and in particular for relational database management.

The relational model

The original ideas are in a seminal paper by Ted Codd entitled A Relational Model of Data for Large Shared Data Banks, which appeared in the Communications of the ACM in June 1970. Codd worked for IBM at the time and spent a number of years refining the ideas in collaboration with a variety of people at IBM, possibly the most influential being Chris Date, who has written extensively on the whole database area. Structured Query Language (SQL) was an outcome of the work of a number of people at IBM. The ANSI Database Committee (X3H2) worked on a standard relational database language and adopted SQL as the basis of its work. SQL has been adopted by the American National Standards Institute, and the ISO will follow. A growing number of commercial manufacturers have adopted SQL and there is now a range of SQL-based products on offer.

A relational database stores data in individual tables. The tables are linked by data in common columns making it possible to combine data from several tables as required.

The following is my home page:

- http://www.kcl.ac.uk/kis/support/cit//fortran/database/database.html

and there are links there to a number of short documents including

- An Overview of Database Management Systems
- An Introduction to the Relational Model.

The primary emphasis of the information is on handling scientific data. The data is mainly environmental as I've worked for both the United Nations Environmental Programme and been the database administrator for an EEC-funded study into environmental kidney damage due to exposure to lead and cadmium.

MySQL

Home page is

- http://www.mysql.com/

MySQL is a relational database management system. The SQL part of MySQL should be obvious! MySQL is Open Source Software. Anybody can download it from the Internet and use it without paying anything. MySQL is fast, reliable and relatively easy to use. You do need a background obviously in the relational model and SQL. References are given in the bibliography

High-performance computing

Scientists and engineers have always been interested in supercomputers and high-performance computing since the first computers arrived in the 1950s. However powerful the computers at their disposal they want more memory, faster processors, and bigger and faster disks. The latter part of the 20th century has seen the development of systems from off-the-shelf components and in 1994 Thomas Sterling and Donald Becker at NASA's Centre of Excellence in Space Data and Information Sciences (CESDIS) built a 16-node network of workstations based on the Intel DX4 processor. It used channel-bonded Ethernet cards to glue everything together. They used message-passing software to build an effective parallel-processing computer on a small budget. They called the system Beowulf.

Parallel programming and high-performance computing

Have a look at:

- http://suparum.rz.uni-mannheim.de/docs/ind.html

for a lot of links to supercomputing centres and information on parallel computing in general.

For details of the US Accelerated Strategic Computing Initiative – ASCI – visit:

- http://www.sandia.gov/ASCI/
- http://www.lanl.gov/projects/asci/asci.html
- http://www.llnl.gov/asci/

The following are some useful UK sites:

- http://www.epsrc.ac.uk/hpc
- http://www.csar.cfs.ac.uk/

The following site lists the top 500 supercomputers in the world:

- http://www.netlib.org/benchmark/top500.html

To see what can be done with all this processing power visit:

- http://www.met-office.gov.uk/

Linux is not the only operating system that can be used and the following

- http://www.ncsa.uiuc.edu/SCD/Hardware/

shows what has been done at The National Center for Super-computing Applications (NCSA), one of the five original centres in the National Science Foundation's Supercomputer Centers Program and a unit of the University of Illinois at Urbana-Champaign using Windows NT.

The following link has details of a High-Performance

Computing Summer School in Linux for HPC held at Manchester University in September 2000:

- http://www.man.ac.uk/mrccs/summer_school/2000/index.shtml

which had people from the UK, Europe and the USA.

Linux clusters

A good place to start is the book by Spector. Details are given in the bibliography. The book has a good historical coverage of supercomputing and chapters on

- Basic computing concepts
- Designing clusters
- Building clusters
- Software installation and configuration
- Managing clusters.

It finishes off with coverage of tools and libraries for parallel programming.

Bibliography

Costales, B. with Allman, E., *Sendmail*, 2nd Edition, O'Reilly

- Excellent coverage of sendmail for the more inquisitive reader.

Spector, D.H.M., *Building Linux Clusters*, O'Reilly

- Good introduction to the subject.

Cannan, S.& Otten, G., *SQL The Standard Handbook*, McGraw Hill.

- Very good coverage of the SQL standard.

Date, C. with Darwen, H., *A Guide to the SQL Standard*, Addison Wesley.

- Date has been involved in relational database management for a long time.

Pratt, P.J., *A Guide to SQL*, Boyd and Fraser

- Good simple guide to SQL.

Resume

The chapter looks at where to go next.

Hopefully you now have a fully working Linux system and you have done enough to appreciate some of the potential of what Unix and Linux have to offer.

You've probably also got very frustrated at times when things don't work. Perseverance is a great help with all aspects of computing, not just Linux.

It probably isn't very productive to regard Windows and Unix/Linux as competing. A computer system is just a tool and you should use the best tool for the job. Some of your work is probably done best on a PC running Windows, some is best done on a Linux system.

Other systems are available and much general-purpose computing and supercomputing is done on systems running Unix. An investment in Linux pays off fairly quickly if you intend to use computers as part of your work.

Bibliography

There are loads of pointers throughout the text. By now you are hopefully getting familiar with working with the on-line material installed on your system, and also in using what the Web has to offer. This is an invaluable resource.

You've also probably come to appreciate that much of computing is RTFM.

Appendix

The exact set of commands that you have available will vary with the distribution. If you go back to chapter 7 and have a look at the recommendations for the File System Hierarchy Standard you will see that the key directories are:

- /bin
- /usr/bin
- /sbin
- /usr/sbin.

The following table summarizes the number of entries in each of these directories for several versions of Linux.

	SuSe		Redhat	
	6.4	7.0	6.2	7.0
/bin	87	93	83	
/usr/bin	841	1988	1630	
/sbin	183	156	151	
/usr/sbin	174	299	151	

The following are the common commands from the SuSe 6.4 and Redhat 7.0 /bin directory.

arch	ash	Shell	ash.static	awk
basename	bash	cat	chgrp	chmod
chown	cp	csh	date	dd
df	dmesg	dnsdomainname	domainname	echo
egrep	false	gawk	grep	gtar
gunzip	gzip	hostname	kill	ln
loadkeys	login	ls	mail	mkdir
mknod	mktemp	more	mount	mv
netstat	nisdomainname	ping	ps	pwd
rm	rmdir	rpm	sed	sh
sleep	stty	su	sync	tar
tcsh	touch	true	umount	uname
vi	ypdomainname	zcat		

Index